T0323989

Cambridge Elements

Elements in Race, Ethnicity, and Politics
edited by
Megan Ming Francis
University of Washington

HOW TO BUILD A DEMOCRACY

From Fannie Lou Hamer and Barbara Jordan to Stacey Abrams

Christina M. Greer
Fordham University

CAMBRIDGE
UNIVERSITY PRESS

Shaftesbury Road, Cambridge CB2 8EA, United Kingdom

One Liberty Plaza, 20th Floor, New York, NY 10006, USA

477 Williamstown Road, Port Melbourne, VIC 3207, Australia

314–321, 3rd Floor, Plot 3, Splendor Forum, Jasola District Centre,
New Delhi – 110025, India

103 Penang Road, #05–06/07, Visioncrest Commercial, Singapore 238467

Cambridge University Press is part of Cambridge University Press & Assessment,
a department of the University of Cambridge.

We share the University's mission to contribute to society through the pursuit of
education, learning and research at the highest international levels of excellence.

www.cambridge.org
Information on this title: www.cambridge.org/9781009500807

DOI: 10.1017/9781009030311

When citing this work, please include a reference to the DOI 10.1017/9781009030311

First published 2024

A catalogue record for this publication is available from the British Library

ISBN 978-1-009-50080-7 Hardback
ISBN 978-1-009-01568-4 Paperback
ISSN 2633-0423 (online)
ISSN 2633-0415 (print)

Cambridge University Press & Assessment has no responsibility for the persistence
or accuracy of URLs for external or third-party internet websites referred to in this
publication and does not guarantee that any content on such websites is, or will
remain, accurate or appropriate.

How to Build a Democracy

From Fannie Lou Hamer and Barbara Jordan to Stacey Abrams

Elements in Race, Ethnicity, and Politics

DOI: 10.1017/9781009030311
First published online: October 2024

Christina M. Greer
Fordham University

Author for correspondence: Christina M. Greer, cgreer@fordham.edu

Abstract: From the toils of Fannie Lou Hamer and Barbara Jordan emerges a twenty-first-century leader, Stacey Abrams. This Element explores the strategic organizing acumen of Fannie Lou Hamer in Mississippi and across the South, and the rise of Barbara Jordan, the second Black woman elected to the House of Representatives and the first Black woman from the US South to head to Congress. The leadership skills and collective political efforts of these two women paved the way for the emergence of Stacey Abrams, a candidate for governor of Georgia in 2018 and 2022, and the organizer of an electoral movement that helped deliver the 2020 presidential victory and US Senate majority to the Democratic Party. This Element adds to the existing literature by framing Black women as integral to the expansion of new voters into the Democratic Party, American democracy, and to the political development of Black people in the US South.

Keywords: Fannie Lou Hamer, Barbara Jordan, Stacey Abrams, US South, Black women

ISBNs: 9781009500807 (HB), 9781009015684 (PB), 9781009030311 (OC)
ISSNs: 2633-0423 (online), 2633-0415 (print)

Contents

1 Introduction

I met Stacey Abrams in early 2018 when she was first running for governor of Georgia. We met in New York through mutual political friends who insisted that I meet "the most dynamic politician" they had ever encountered. Like many people at that time, I did not see how a Georgia governor's race had much to do with me in New York City. I did not think the state was ready for a Black governor, a female governor, and definitely not a Black female governor. Yet after hearing Stacey Abrams speak for five minutes, I knew she could and most likely would be the next governor of the state of Georgia. Her understanding of Georgia as a compilation of urban, suburban, and rural locales, her inclusion of Asian Americans and Latinx residents in her analysis of political incorporation, and her pragmatic approach to governance and coalition building further highlighted the brilliant tactical skills that millions of Americans have come to know. The nation slowly began to recognize Abrams as the orator, tactician, and policy specialist who possessed the leadership skills to be governor . . . or even president. A type of hagiography formed around the legend that was Abrams, but her skill set, leadership skills, coalition building with Democrats (and even Republicans), and intellectual understanding of politics and policy extended beyond the myth of Black girl electoral magic. What were her political roots that made her stand so tall and so strong in the face of egregious Republican onslaughts?

Journalists and pundits asked where a woman like Abrams came from. How was she able to help secure three crucial Democratic wins and change the course of history?[1] Journalists focus their (positive) press coverage of white candidates at greater rates than Blacks running for office (Hicks, 2022). However, Abrams garnered more media coverage than her initial white challenger in 2018 and continued to draw fascination, admiration, and admonition from news outlets throughout Georgia and the nation. Despite the negative stereotyping of Abrams, her brand of straight talk, coupled with nuanced and relatable policy breakdowns, garnered the support of a diverse sector of the electorate (Hicks, 2022).

Abrams was merely following a long lineage of Black women from the US South who organized outside the electoral space and voted within the electoral realm in order to maximize their collective presence, despite the four pillars of American democracy: racialized capitalism, white supremacy, anti-Black racism, and patriarchy (hooks, 1997). Much of the media portrays Abrams as a superwoman-type figure who swooped down and saved the country (and

---

[1] Abrams helped organize voters in Georgia, which helped deliver the state to Joe Biden in the 2020 presidential election, as well as two successful Democratic Senate victories in January 2021.

possibly the world) from the reign of President Donald Trump and his allies. However, for those who understand the origins of grassroots organizing and coalition building – as well as the electoral battles won in order to increase the franchise for Black people, women, and, after the 1965 Voting Rights Act (VRA), the rights of Black women more broadly – Abrams did not appear out of nowhere as if from a different planet. She grew out of the soil tilled by Black women throughout the US South who for decades have been doing the work of organizing and mobilizing voters and building multigenerational and multiracial coalitions – in and out of the spotlight – and in and out of the formal political mechanisms.

Stacey Abrams was able to build on the efforts of courageous Black women who came before her, but there are two in particular who stand out: Fannie Lou Hamer and Barbara Jordan. Although the US South has progressed tremendously since Reconstruction, the continued and systemic disenfranchisement of Black voters is palpable across the region. Abrams's efforts to register and educate marginalized Georgians across the state are reminiscent of Hamer's efforts to mobilize rural Mississippians in the face of white supremacists hellbent on excluding Black voters. Abrams's broad coalition building and bipartisan effectiveness in the Georgia statehouse is reminiscent of Jordan's days in the Texas statehouse and Congress. Therefore, if we are to fully understand the success and potential of Stacey Abrams, we must look to these two women as key elements of her political foundation some fifty-plus years after their Herculean efforts. Thus, we have three Black women, all children of the US South, with a deep understanding of politics, policy, and power. Their leadership skills and charisma – which are often ascribed to male leaders, both white and Black – established an archetype of Black female leadership that is rarely seen or understood by society. Most importantly, all three women understood the importance of the Democratic Party and building power on the national level. They built infrastructures to support campaigns and introduce new voters to electoral politics. And they refused to back down even after setbacks rooted in inherent American anti-Blackness.

I was determined to figure out just who were Abrams's direct political predecessors. Abrams reminded me of Hamer, another daughter of the US South known for her oratorical prowess who was able to move hearts, minds, and policy with her passion for justice and her understanding of the promises of American democracy. Abrams, too, could stir a room with a story of justice denied, whether her own or a fellow citizen's. Hamer was also known for her coalition building with several like-minded individuals and groups in her pursuit of a more just and equitable Mississippi. As she worked tirelessly to ensure that the franchise was extended equally to Black people and other marginalized groups, her bravery and organizing efforts reminded me of Abrams and her tenacity in the pursuit of voting equity in Georgia and beyond. I also realized that Abrams displayed Barbara Jordan–esque political savvy and skills while negotiating with Republicans and Democrats in the Georgia state-house. Abrams was able to consistently gain seats for her party, help pass legislation, and even help block legislation by forming alliances when neces-sary. Her eloquence and skills in the legislative and negotiation processes reminded me of Jordan during her tenure in the Texas statehouse and her days negotiating with members of the Congressional Black Caucus (CBC) and white southern Democrats while in Congress. If I combined Fannie Lou Hamer and Barbara Jordan and added half a century, I could better understand Stacey Abrams as a fearless trailblazer in the face of recalcitrant white supremacy, a leader in strengthening voting rights, and a skillful legislator and negotiator.

I am aware that there are countless other Black women who could be chronicled in this Element, side by side with Hamer, Jordan, and Abrams. There are Black women who blazed trails in electoral and organizational politics from all regions of the United States. However, I chose to put these three women in conversation with one another. All hail from the South; all three overcame outsider statuses to lead a new conversation about Black politics, Democratic politics, and Black female leadership; and all three held fearless negotiations to advance inclusion and equity for Black people and other mar-ginalized groups. All three changed the way the Democratic Party infrastructure organized itself, built multiracial coalitions, ran campaigns, and even selected candidates. Abrams's transition from minority leader in the Georgia statehouse to the Democratic nominee for governor, and potentially the first-ever Black woman elected governor in the United States was a national movement that rested on the oratorical skills of Hamer and Jordan, the organizing principles and prowess of Hamer, and the political acumen of Jordan. The common denominator among all three women is their ability to articulate a vision of political inclusion and electoral mobilization for Black Americans and other marginalized groups that have yet to experience full inclusion into the Democratic Party, American democracy, and the American Dream.

The crux of this Element rests on the central belief that protest and electoral politics are essential in order for democracy in America to become a reality. As active participants in building a more inclusive nation, Black Americans must employ a "both/and" approach in that both electoral and protest politics must be utilized to gain and maintain attention for policies of import (Tate, 1998). This dual approach is what has led to the success of Stacey Abrams, someone willing to work within the electoral sphere as well as utilize "outsider" politics in the activist and organizing spaces to lay another foundation for equity and inclusion of Black people and other marginalized groups. By chronicling the efforts of Hamer, Jordan, and Abrams, we are able to better understand the expansion of democracy, the Democratic Party, and the political development of Black people in the South, and America more broadly. The intra- and interparty efforts of Hamer and Jordan directly contribute to the multipronged strategy employed by Abrams nearly a half century later.

The contributions of Black women to protest politics and behind-the-scenes organizing are becoming more evident in the scholarship of historians, political scientists, and sociologists as they document the ways Black women organized their local communities, raised money, and educated their peers about political processes and policies (Jones, 2020; Smooth, 2011). However, Black women's entrée into the electoral space as candidates has not been as robust as that of Black men (Gillespie, 2012), largely because of constraints pertaining to fundraising, feeder occupations, and the belief that Black women could not lead on a local, state, or national level (Brown, 2014). These beliefs were often held by those assumed to be allies in these endeavors. In the 1960s and 1970s, when the women's rights movement was looking for candidates, Black women stepped up and said they were present and ready to lead. The implicit assumption was that *woman* meant *white woman*, thus further pushing Black women to the sidelines, as evidenced by much of the initial academic literature of "women" in politics (Greer, 2016a; Slaughter et al., 2024). Much of the academic literature on women in politics was a white-centered analysis that ignored the contributions and existence of nonwhite political actors. Even the initial research on the so-called gender gap failed to take race into account (Howell and Day, 2000; Kaufmann, 2006; Wirls, 1986). Had it done so, the literature would have presented a much clearer picture of the ways that race trumped gender in analyses of white women in the electoral sphere (Junn, 2017).

Similarly, during this time, when Black men were thinking of running in high-profile races and espousing the need for Black leadership on the ticket, yet again, Black women stepped forward to say they were present and ready to lead. Often, however, they were pushed to the sidelines because implicit in the request for Black leadership was a need for Black *men* to lead (Chisholm, [1970] 2009; Greer, 2016a; Smooth, 2011) – thus creating a political no-man's-land for Black women, who were not thought of as female leaders or as Black leaders when mainstream conversations about increasing diverse leadership and electoral representation were had.

We cannot understand the success and drive of Stacey Abrams without understanding the longer history of Fannie Lou Hamer and Barbara Jordan. Hamer is finally getting her due as an organizer, strategist, and coalition builder in her efforts to secure voting rights for Black people across the US South, beginning in segregated Mississippi. Jordan is best known for her intellectual prowess and eloquence as an elected official and member of the US House of Representatives. Analyzing the willingness of both women to work with other Black women and with organizers to accomplish their respective goals helps us better understand who Abrams is, the political lineage from which she descends, and her foundation as an elected official and organizer.

Essentially, Hamer and Jordan embody a type of protest and electoral politics that, when combined with coalition-building politics and voter mobilization, contributes to the foundation that helps bring forth a twenty-first-century leader in Abrams, who is both a politician and an organizer. Hamer's ability to organize and build coalitions across groups in the United States contributed to her success in pushing for change inside electoral politics while using outsider political tactics. Jordan's ability to persevere and excel in an electoral space in the Deep South contributed to her success as a legislator, an oratorical leader, and a multiracial coalition builder within the Democratic Party. Because of this multidimensional approach to Black politics, gender politics, and electoral and organizing politics, we can better understand the current political moment for Black Americans, and Black women more specifically. It is also impossible to understand the threats to our current democratic circumstance if we do not understand the roles that Black women played inside and outside the electoral space and develop a more nuanced picture of the past and current political climate and the history of the US South.

There are several different modern-day narratives of "democracy saving" in American politics. Some authors have focused on Ruth Bader Ginsburg or the efforts of feminist organizers (Eschle, 2001; Hinojosa and Kittilson, 2020; Kaplan, 2004; Lithwick, 2019). Others have focused on Black politics more broadly and the role of Black electeds on the local level, the significance of Barack Obama's presidency, or statewide elected officials (Gillespie, 2010). However, the story of Black American women in the South, utilizing local political strategies to help reimagine national Democratic politics, past and present, is a story that still needs to be told. Indeed, there are detailed stories and important historiographies of Hamer and Jordan (Blain, 2021; Bracey, 2011; Kammer, 2016; Larson, 2021; Lee, 1999; Rogers, 1998). However, it is important to tell the story of Hamer, Jordan, and Abrams in unison as we better understand the institutions that support, and disrupt, American democracy. The broad impact of these three women as contributors to the larger US democratic project must be examined beyond highlighting the accomplishments of Black men as foundational to American institutions and democracy. By observing these three women together, we can move closer to a more wholistic picture of the triumphs and challenges of American democracy and party politics, past and present.

There are two key elements to our understanding of the significance of these three women. First is the importance of region. The US South has been the foundation and starting point in the origin story for much of Black America. States that sanctioned and promoted chattel slavery on their land represent a distinct part of US history that cannot be ignored or erased. As Black America diversifies by ethnicity and within geographic locales across the United States, we cannot ignore the persistent significance of the South if we want to understand Black–white relations and how past practices have been incorporated into modern-day behaviors and levels of honesty about the horrors that occurred on US soil. The second is the role of Black women as leaders and politicians. The United States has a long and robust history of Black female leaders, but the history of Black women as politicians has not been as long-standing because of the institutional barriers of race and gender. Although the number of Black female politicians may not be commensurate with those of their Black male and white female counterparts, the reality of Black women as leaders in their respective communities and as defenders of American democracy for generations cannot be denied (Brown, 2014; Brown and Gershon, 2016; Stokes-Brown and Dolan, 2010).

What makes these three women so important in our understanding of American democracy is their ability to identify the oftentimes unyielding power of the four pillars of racialized capitalism – racialized capitalism, white supremacy, anti-Black racism, and patriarchy – yet steadfastly work to dismantle them. What I aim to do in this Element is dissect the ways in which these three women on the one hand felt as if these pillars were oftentimes immovable obstacles, and yet on the other hand were motivated to begin to chip away at said obstacles. It is unclear whether these foundational characteristics of American democracy are capable of ever being removed or even eroded. However, the steadfast efforts by these three women to change what has often seemed impervious to change is what makes them the unique leaders and beacons of American patriotism that they are. It is their belief in the possibility of this change that further persuades me that their efforts were not in vain and that their leadership and coalition efforts can actually move this country closer to its stated (and not yet fully practiced) ideals. The common thread connecting the lives of these three women is their persistence and their belief in American democracy and its ability to change. All three women at their core have a pragmatic view of this country's ability to move beyond its original practices and closer to the ideals and principles stated in its founding documents.

What Are the Stakes?

We are in a precarious moment in our democracy, when long-fought battles that seemed to have been won are now literally being relitigated in courts across the country. Statehouses are deciding how to punish teachers, maintain segregated schooling, and roll back voting rights and the rights of women to have autonomy over their own bodies. Essentially, basic civil rights and civil liberties are being eroded by conservative legislators and judges and threatening to erase much of the progress that was hard fought for and won by women like Jordan, Hamer, and Abrams. As the country continues to address the fallout of four years of a Republican president who actively worked against democratic principles, inclusion of people of color and immigrants, a stronger social safety net, and environmental and educational concerns of families in cities and suburbs across the country, it was consistently Black women who called the president and the Republican Party to task.

Underlying much of this research has been an attempt to answer succinctly and concretely why Black women matter in an electoral space. When directed at leaders in Black political thought, the academic and public focus is often on Black men (Gillespie, 2010). This project centers three Black women, and Black women more broadly, and their contributions to electoral and protest politics, local and national politics, and participation and inclusion in campaigns and elections past, present, and future. As Black women navigate persistent gender inequities and long-standing racial biases and exclusion while attempting to course-correct centuries of behaviors, policies, and an overall ethos of a nation, their role as the keepers and saviors of democracy becomes more evident. Clearly, Abrams did not act alone. It was the organizing efforts of Abrams, in addition to the work of several grassroots groups and the participation of so many Black female voters in key states, that led mainstream media to recognize the power of Black women to assist the nation in living up to the ideals of its founding principles (Bunch, 2021).

As many focused on the election of Kamala Harris as the first nonwhite, nonmale US vice president (Goodyear, 2020; Lerner and Ember, 2020), I was interested in thinking about Abrams – a qualified Black woman with deep roots in the US South who was not selected as vice president – and the Black American women's shoulders upon whom Abrams stands.

Building on the legacy of Hamer and Jordan, Abrams is a Black American woman from the South who has been unafraid to build intra- and interparty coalitions. When thinking of why Abrams is important to this moment, we can discuss her role, in what many have argued is saving American democracy in the 2020 election (Bunch, 2021). Abrams, as founder of Fair Fight, worked to increase voter registration and education in Georgia and other key states across the nation, thus contributing to incumbent president Donald Trump's defeat. The efforts by Abrams also highlighted the work of countless organizations to increase voter awareness, registration, and participation, all while state legislatures and state courts were taking away inclusive electoral practices for people of color, poor people, and immigrants. A key element of Abrams's success in her statehouse elections, campaigning, and most especially in her pursuits since the 2018 election has been her ability to build substantive coalitions. Like Fannie Lou Hamer, who built bridges with other civil rights groups throughout the South and with civil rights leaders throughout the country, Abrams saw the need to form alliances with groups doing similar work to effect change.

As we assess the political imagination and work of Black women, inside the realms of both electoral politics and protest politics, it is abundantly clear that Abrams not only has a cadre of Black female organizers and electeds with whom she works but also hails from a long legacy of Black women who have worked to help realize a truer American democracy through time (Waxman, 2020). For example, the organizational and registration efforts of Fannie Lou Hamer introduced marginalized Black voters to electoral politics. Her work with the Student Nonviolent Coordinating Committee (SNCC) created a new class of voters as well as a foundation for new generations of voters in the US South. Hamer's recognition of the importance of grassroots organizing and local politics, under the mentorship of Ella Baker, helped sow the seeds of political participation for Black southerners, a population that has always had a tenuous relationship with citizenship and the franchise due to the deep roots of white supremacy and anti-Black racism. Fast-forward several decades, and Abrams employed similar strategies – sadly, under similar constraints – to increase voter registration and participation in states across the nation.

The Significance of the US South

The South holds a unique place in America's origin story. Due to centuries of chattel slavery of Africans in America, the Civil War, and Reconstruction efforts, the South encapsulates the complexities surrounding the Black–white binary and the calcified notions of white supremacy and anti-Black racism (Du Bois, [1935] 1998; Foner, 2014). The violent history of the South continues to play out today. Home to the majority of Black Americans, historically and in the present day, the South holds the brutal history of centuries of Black American bondage. It is also the region where Black Americans have been fighting oppressive apartheid-like regimes on local levels for centuries. Violent, racist practices such as lynching were just one of the ways that whites maintained racial order in the South. Black people who dared to transcend the racial order that placed them at the bottom of the political, social, and economic structure in the United States were often met with brutal consequences that endangered their overall well-being, livelihoods, and lives (Chafe et al., 2011; Clarke, 1998; Painter, 2021).

Although organizing efforts were often met with brutal (and sometimes deadly) consequences, Black Americans continued to fight for their freedom and equality. Blacks in the South, and in America more broadly, have fought for the values of a nation that has yet to live up to its full ideals and potential. The political exclusion of Black people by whites in power in the US South has been (and continues to be) a deliberate endeavor. À la carte racism was directed at Black men, women, and children in all facets of their lives, and the US South continues to be an overt epicenter for the racist ideals of a significant number of white elected officials and their voters. So why is the US South unique, and why do we need to explicitly think about Black female politicians and organizers to better understand Black politics? Southern legislatures used legal and extralegal measures to dilute and/or eliminate the Black vote, resulting in limited participation by Black Americans in southern politics before the passage of the VRA of 1965 (Grant, 2020).

The US South is a necessary focal point because for many one would assume it is the last place for Black women to have political power. Therefore, the fact that Hamer, Jordan, and Abrams all successfully organized, built coalitions, increased electoral participation, and challenged the dominant power structure in various ways is worthy of more detailed exploration. The US South featured prominently in the identities of all three women in their political lives. Racism exists throughout the entire United States; however, there is a certain brand of Confederate racism that has always made the South different from other regions of the country. Hamer knew all too well the blatant brutality that existed in the South. Violence toward Black citizens occurred in major cities in every state, but the South was where rampant brutality from the state, as well as vigilantes, was allowed – and even encouraged – in order to maintain the racial order of the time. Jordan saw the alliances and compromises that Texas Democrats made with their fellow Republicans to maintain the racial order. Even her friend and mentor President Lyndon Johnson would compromise with his fellow Texas and other southern Democrats at times so as not to disturb the white nationalist leanings of the region and his home state. And Abrams ran for office during a time of a diversifying South, one that moved from the Black–white binary to a more racially and ethnically diverse region. However, the uphill battle convincing voters – Black, white, and other – that a Black woman could run and actually win in a southern state was a feat so large, it gained national and international attention.

How to Build a Democracy: Fannie Lou Hamer, Barbara Jordan, and Stacey Abrams

There are several unifying features of the three women in this Element. All three had self-sacrificing and resourceful parents, and all three used insider and outsider political tactics for coalition building in order to help them better assess and amass political power. All three possessed leadership qualities that helped advance policy goals pertaining to electoral inclusion and increased voting rights for Black people and other groups in the United States. Fannie Lou Hamer grew up in the Jim Crow South, Barbara Jordan in the segregated South, and Stacey Abrams in the post–Jim Crow and legally segregated South, but still in a society with de facto and de jure racism and segregation. All three women understood the limitations placed on women, Black people, and especially Black women. Therefore, in order to advance their varying political agendas, they relied on networks of relationship cultivation with other individuals and organizations to assist in their freedom-building and political efforts. Hamer worked with various civil rights organizations throughout the US South in order to enact policy changes in southern states. Jordan worked with colleagues, both Black and white, in order to pursue economic and political advancement for Black people and diverse groups of Texans more broadly. And Abrams has worked with other organizations in Georgia and across the United States to build a more concrete foundation pertaining to voting rights and equal political opportunities for all. Hamer used her skills as an organizer to change minds and policy by building local coalitions that put external pressure on national elected officials, and Jordan effectively utilized tactics working within the electoral sphere to change minds and policies on local, state, and national levels. As both women worked to increase the electoral participation of Blacks through voting and registration efforts, they understood the power of the ballot and the importance of Black political representation in leadership roles and electoral politics. Abrams's twenty-first-century efforts represent the combined work of Hamer and Jordan. What Abrams did during the two decades before she ran for the Georgia governorship is an amalgamation of legal study, grassroots organizing, economic uplift for Black communities, and the attainment of electoral office. Abrams is the effort of Hamer and Jordan combined and realized.

These three women shared unique traits that have solidified their position in the pantheon of Black America and American history writ large. Through their ability to inspire, communicate, compromise, organize, and move forward an agenda for all Americans, and Black Americans in particular, these three women laid a foundation for a particular type of patriotism never seen before in American electoral and organizational politics. The similarities among these three daughters of the US South extend beyond their leadership skills and oratorical excellence. Abrams has utilized the Hamer strategies of grassroots organizing and the Jordan tactics of intra- and interparty coalition building that were so crucial to the electoral successes of these two predecessors more than fifty years ago. Like Hamer in Mississippi, Abrams has worked with groups throughout Georgia to educate and include marginalized citizens and turn them into voters. And just as Jordan used her political office to push forward legislation that would lead to a more inclusive body politic, Abrams, as Georgia House minority leader, used her bully pulpit to advocate on behalf of marginalized people throughout the state. What is unique about Abrams is her ability and willingness to maintain a firm commitment to grassroots politics while also serving in an electoral capacity. For Abrams, it was never either/or when it came to protest and electoral politics, but a marriage of the two strategies in order to advance her policy agenda in the twenty-first century, especially as it pertained to voting rights, equity, and inclusion.

Racialized capitalism, white supremacy, anti-Black racism, and patriarchy have always served as limitations for Black female leaders, and Fannie Lou Hamer, Barbara Jordan, and Stacey Abrams were not exempt. Yet, despite the calcified inequities that are part of the American foundation, Hamer, Jordan, and Abrams found ways to negotiate these limitations into a new electoral and organizational space for Black people in the US South. The effects of their efforts not only are long-standing but also permeated beyond southern politics and into the Democratic Party and American electorate more broadly. Over the past sixty years, Black women have worked within the established political framework, in which they are often treated as the least deserving and last in line for the full benefits of the American polity.

All three women shared the belief that the government exists to provide for people. That same government must also provide those freedoms and protections, and goods and services, equally. All three women fought (and continue to fight, in Abrams's case) for the dignity of Black people in America. Through this patriotic exercise, their efforts have been felt across racial and ethnic groups in the United States.

The central argument of *How to Build a Democracy* is that Fannie Lou Hamer, Barbara Jordan, and Stacey Abrams changed the face of the Democratic Party and contributed to greater enfranchisement for Black Americans specifically, and all Americans more broadly, by increasing party infrastructure and building coalitions across race and region. By failing to take into account the collective contributions of these three Black women, and countless other Black women who have contributed to the process of democracy building, we fail to see the larger process of American political development and Democratic Party building. Which elements of American democracy and the democratic process do we miss when we fail to examine how the contributions of Hamer and Jordan laid the foundation for Abrams, arguably one of the most important politicians of the twenty-first century? Abrams is rightfully credited with strengthening Black politics and broadening American democracy in the South and across the nation. By further interrogating the struggles, contributions, and successes of these three women, we can better understand the complicated ebbs and flows of democracy in the United States. By analyzing the contributions of these three women, we can better understand the tools needed for this current political moment, when Republican leaders are attempting to roll back legislation to pre-1960s policies. What can we learn from the strategies and organizing principles of Hamer and Jordan to help guide the country through the current moment of political division and the reemergence of racist policies against Black people and other marginalized groups?

Through the years, scores of Black women have tilled US soil through electoral office at local, state, and federal levels. Ella Baker, Septima Clark, Gloria Richardson, and Rosa Parks are a small sampling of the Black women who organized outside of the electoral space to pressure elected officials to change or create legislation for the advancement of Black people, which in turn has been an investment in *all* Americans and this democratic project. Stacey Abrams arrived some fifty years later and not only tilled the soil prepared for her by Fannie Lou Hamer but also began to plant her own seeds to further American democracy and the larger project of creating a more equitable democratic republic for all – not just Black Americans, not just those in the South, not just Democrats, and not just those on the margins. She was fighting for the inclusion of Americans excluded from the electoral and democratic ideals of America.

The election of Barbara Jordan to the House of Representatives in 1972 as the first Black woman from the US South opened the doors of possibility for Black women in electoral politics for generations to come – from mayors to leaders in the statehouse to representatives in Congress, and ultimately to Stacey Abrams as a credible candidate for governor of Georgia. Other trailblazing Black women in Congress like Yvonne Brathwaite Burke and Shirley Chisholm freed the imaginations of subsequent generations of Black women in electoral politics. Following their historic elections, Black women ran for local and state office across the country, thus providing a new understanding of descriptive and substantive politics.

Patriotism is often defined as love of one's country and steadfast loyalty to it as a homeland and to its values, and pride in its ideals and principles (Johnson, 2018). Upon review of the efforts of Hamer, Jordan, and Abrams, it is undeniable that these three Black women articulated a type of US southern patriotism based first on the protection and advancement of Black people. Their southern roots – steeped in chattel slavery, failed Reconstruction efforts, Jim Crow practices, and varying forms of segregation – gave each of them a unique view of the capacity and limitations of party politics, institutions, and the United States more broadly. This view helped them gain the best understanding of how to maneuver the political minefields ahead. A nation predicated on anti-Black racism and patriarchy is not a place or space established for the advancement of Black women, yet Hamer and Jordan were able to plant extraordinary seeds within the political realm.

This Element contributes to our understanding of these three Black women specifically as contributors to the progress of Black politics in the last sixty years, the challenges they faced, the obstacles they overcame, and the progress they made for Black voters in America. *How to Build a Democracy* adds to the existing literature by framing Black women in politics as integral to understanding the Democratic Party, the expansion of American democracy, and the political development of Black people in the US South. Furthermore, it adds to American political literature by emphasizing Black women electeds as insiders, outsiders, power brokers, and change makers who have contributed to the ways in which we understand democracy and Democratic politics in the latter twentieth and early twenty-first centuries.

Outline of the Element

The sections that follow describe the impact of Black women on electoral politics in the US South in the states of Mississippi, Texas, and Georgia. Section 2 details Fannie Lou Hamer's blending of organizational, economic, and electoral politics. Hamer's efforts can best be described as outsider-turned insider in electoral politics. This section details Hamer's registration efforts across Mississippi and her work with SNCC. Hamer joined other Black female organizers who helped educate sharecroppers, domestics, and other Black people, who by and large were ignored by dominant party politics. Not only did Hamer challenge the institutional structures of the Democratic Party, but she did so by organizing Black people through the Mississippi Freedom Democratic Party (MFDP). By building a multiracial coalition in the US South, Hamer and her colleagues established a model that challenged institutional structures in Mississippi, across the South, and even in Washington, DC. This section also provides the reader with a better understanding of the impact Hamer had on the 1964 Democratic National Convention (DNC) and the future of the Democratic Party, then known as an all-white party with ancillary Black support and leadership. Who was this daughter of sharecroppers, and how did she capture the attention of the nation with her riveting and brutal honesty about the trials and tribulations of Black people in the US South? How did this woman without formal education become one of the leading voices of the Civil Rights Movement and advanced the registration efforts of thousands of Black people in America?

Section 3 describes the political efforts of Barbara Jordan as a member of the House of Representatives and her effect on national politics. The section engages Jordan's strategy and eloquence to discuss how and why she was an effective legislator during and after her time in office. First, I assert that her Texas roots enabled her to be an integral part of the CBC and yet autonomous at the same time as a southerner. Some of the literature on Black electeds focuses on representation from a northern urban perspective and omits the contributions and challenges of Black representatives from the US South. Instead of focusing on the limitations placed on Jordan as one of the few Black members of the House of Representatives during her tenure in Washington, DC, I take the position that Jordan was able to influence democratic and Democratic Party politics in covert and overt ways. In other words, I question how one woman changed the course of presidential and party politics even with the intersectional challenges of race and gender. Furthermore, I consider the contributions of Jordan as an important explanation for the changing politics of the US South.

Section 4 examines the organizational and political efforts of Stacey Abrams in the state of Georgia, roughly fifty years after Fannie Lou Hamer famously became the voice of registration efforts of Black southerners and Barbara Jordan was first elected to the House of Representatives. This section chronicles the electoral successes of Abrams during her tenure in the Georgia statehouse, her grassroots organizing across Georgia, and the historic 2018 Georgia guber-natorial race. I detail the individual successes of Abrams, her coalition-building efforts with other Black women and groups across Georgia, and the subsequent institutional changes made at the state level. Although Abrams's 2018 electoral bid was riddled with disenfranchisement of Black and Democratic voters by her opponent and the statewide Republican Party, her consistent grassroots efforts that led up to and continued after the 2018 election laid the foundation for Democratic victories in Georgia in the 2020 presidential election and in two statewide US Senate seats. Abrams's contributions to the Democratic Party and democracy writ large had rippling effects beyond Georgia and the rest of the US South. Her mobilizing efforts also exposed the calcified inequities in the registration and voting processes in the American political system for the national and international communities to see.

The Element's conclusion asks the question, "So where do we go from here?" The civil rights era produced not only Fannie Lou Hamer and Barbara Jordan but also other Black women who were elected to local positions, statehouses, and Congress from the South and major American cities across the nation. The conclusion introduces us to a new way of thinking about the bridge that connects Hamer and Jordan to Abrams, the importance of Black American women to the American electorate and the Democratic Party, and the contemporary impact of Black women as candidates and voters in US politics. Each election cycle Black women run for elected office. Black women have begun financially supporting candidates for office, organizing their communities for formal and informal party politics, and highlighting the persistent inequities in the American electoral system. This new era of Black politics is being led by Black women, sustained by Black women, and saved by Black women. The careers of Hamer, Jordan, and Abrams raise questions about the limitations of Black women in politics, the importance of region in one's ability to make substantive change in national party politics, and how Black female candidates and voters should proceed politically in a nation predicated on white supremacy, anti-Black racism, patriarchy, and racialized capitalism. Thus, the conclusion further dissects the national political impact of these three southern women and their brand of organizing, coalition politics, and registration efforts on modern-day Black politics.

The story of America is one of progress and regress, and a steady effort of Black Americans to help right the wrongs of the past. The story of American politics is a story of protest and politics, the reliance on one for the advancement of the other. The history of race and racism has inextricably linked Black Americans over time and across class and geographic space (Brown-Dean, 2019; Dawson, 1994; Grant, 2020). This Element is an attempt to contextualize Fannie Lou Hamer and Barbara Jordan, just two of the Black American women who led Black politics in the mid-twentieth century, and the seeds they helped plant for the emergence of another Black woman, Stacey Abrams, who used their tools to work with others both inside and outside electoral politics. If this country is ever to change, it will take consistent efforts, and hopefully the responsibility will not fall squarely on the shoulders of Black women. However, until other groups collectively understand what is at stake, we must heed the words of Audre Lorde and remember that "revolution is not a one-time event." These three women worked tirelessly to uproot the American foundation of racialized capitalism, white supremacy, anti-Black racism, and patriarchy and should be understood as the canaries in the coal mine who alert others to the dangers ahead and assist us in strategizing for the future.

2 Fannie Lou Hamer: Ain't Gonna Let Nobody Turn Me 'Round

Leaders of the Civil Rights Movement, American democracy, and freedom movements are not often portrayed as women, descendants of sharecroppers and US chattel slavery, or people without formal educational training. However, Fannie Lou Hamer's fight for political and economic freedom left an indelible mark on America. A woman who endured poverty and racism at almost every turn of her life, as the last and twentieth child of Mississippi sharecroppers, Hamer endured the indignities of being poor, Black, and a woman in the Deep South. The sexual violence and forced sterilization at the hands of white southerners that she experienced as an adult not only shaped her passion for Black freedom struggles but also instilled in her a style of leadership not previously seen before in American politics (Berry and Gross, 2020; Blain, 2021; Brooks, 2020; Lee, 1999).[2]

Hamer was born in 1917 in Montgomery County, Mississippi, one of the most repressive states for Black people, and one that limited Black electoral participation at almost every turn. Hamer witnessed gross injustices, both economic and political, in her daily life, which led to her journey toward activism. During her upbringing, she observed the abject poverty and daily indignities of Black people around her; more than 80 percent of Black Mississippians lived below the poverty line, and the majority of the Black population were sharecroppers. Access to education was severely limited for Black people, and only 3 percent of Black Mississippians were registered to vote (Berry and Gross, 2020) – not because of disinterest, but because of systemic and institutional barriers to participation. The individual obstacles that Black people faced were the result of white individuals' actions toward them in a system that promoted and supported these racist practices (Colby, 1986; Parker, 2011; Timpone, 1997).

As the former child of sharecroppers, the wife of a sharecropper, and a woman who experienced decades of toil on land owned by white people – under working conditions and for wages that can only be described as cruel and inhumane – Hamer believed that economic independence was another

---

[2] Fannie Lou Hamer experienced a forced sterilization, a procedure that was used so commonly on poor Black women in the Mississippi Delta that it was often referred to as a "Mississippi appendectomy," in that Black women would enter the hospital for a procedure and wake up to find themselves sterilized (Larson, 2021). This was part of a larger sterilization project of poor Black women across the South and was not an uncommon practice.

way for Black people in the Mississippi Delta to attain their freedom from the sometimes all-encompassing weight of white supremacy and economic exclusion in a white-controlled economy (Blain, 2021; Larson, 2021). Hamer understood the power of local grassroots organizations to educate and organize Black people against the oppressive power of white elites and their organized and entrenched systems of oppression. Grassroots organizing provided communities with a level of confidence as well as a sense of purpose. The essence of a true democracy is a system where the people are the true sources of power (Qin, 2023). Hamer embraced the power of people on the ground, no matter their circumstance, to help plant the seeds of change and build power from the ground up. Once Hamer was introduced to the power of grassroots organizing, she focused on the Mississippi Freedom Labor Union, Head Start programs, and the Freedom Farm Cooperative, a cooperative founded by Hamer to house, feed, and clothe Mississippi's poorest individuals and communities (Lee, 1999: x). Hamer's insistence on economic emancipation in conjunction with political incorporation and enfranchisement is the foundation of her legacy.

Political science scholars often analyze political engagement in terms of voting and formal ways that citizens involve themselves in the political process (Lipjhart, 1997; Olsen, 1972; Page and Shapiro, 1993). More formal and traditional forms of political participation are often heralded as the measure of citizen engagement. However, differing measures of diverse forms of political engagement are necessary to best understand how marginalized groups engage in the political process without full access to the ballot or traditional forms of participation (Franklin, 2014; Tate, 1998; Walton, 1985).

Hamer spoke plainly, directly, and unapologetically while organizing various communities and explaining their rights to them and their circumstances with and without the right to vote. Some more-established leaders viewed Hamer as an embarrassment in the world of politics because of her sharecropping background, lack of formal education, and Mississippi Delta speech patterns (Lee, 1999: xi). For Hamer, SNCC was able not only to cultivate and harness local talent, especially local female talent, already present in communities throughout the region, but also to present tangible and relatively short-term goals, such as voter registration efforts. In addition, Hamer was able to have a sense of legitimacy working for and with an established organization that had decided to organize in Mississippi and seek assistance from those Mississippians closest to the problem (Bracey, 2011). The leadership and mentorship of Ella Baker helped lay much of the foundation for Hamer's organizing and coalition building.

Years after Hamer's introduction to SNCC, she would go on to cofound the MFDP to assist Black people entering into the formalized political process.

Even though the Fifteenth Amendment gave Black men the franchise in 1865, the implementation of those rights throughout the United States was slow or nonexistent, especially in the Deep South. Hamer understood the power of the vote and the ability to change one's economic circumstances, political leadership, and overall life chances. If the vote did not change one's circumstances, then why were whites so insistent on keeping the vote from Black people in almost every state, most especially in the Deep South (Franklin, 2014; Parker, 2011; Walton, 1985)?

In national politics, Hamer is best known for her speech at the 1964 DNC in Atlantic City, New Jersey, where she detailed a beating by police in Winona, Mississippi, that left her partially blind.[3] For many in the nation, it was the first time hearing a detailed account of the brutality happening on American soil. Many Americans lived in a nation where they resided comfortably in their presumed separate but equal lifestyle. It was Hamer's detailed account of the daily horrors Black men, women, and children experienced that helped wake up segments of the nation. Sadly, white violence was an all-too-common reality for Black people in the US South who crossed paths with white police in any capacity, guilty or not, activist or not. However, the long-lasting legacy of Hamer extends well beyond the speech that brought her to national (and some would argue international) recognition.

This section explores the political journey of Fannie Lou Hamer and her fight to secure the vote for Blacks in the US South, using insider and outsider tactics to expose local and state inequities to the national public, and ultimately helping to change how Black people saw themselves as political actors. Beginning in the summer of 1962 and her introduction to SNCC, Hamer's entry into the Civil Rights Movement was met with retaliation not only against her but also against her loved ones. The loss of jobs and housing was just one of the struggles the Hamer family endured. Vigilante white violence, bombings, and constant harassment were among the many prices Hamer paid for daring to register to vote and bringing political awareness and bravery to her Mississippi Delta community.

---

[3] For a detailed account of the gruesome beating Hamer and her fellow SNCC organizers endured, see Bracey, 2011: 85–88. The injuries Hamer suffered during her June 1964 beating followed her (and haunted her) for the remainder of her life. The beating was so severe that Hamer suffered from kidney damage as well as a blood clot in her left eye that left her with permanently limited eyesight (Bracey, 2011; Rubel, 1990). These life-altering injuries were sustained when Hamer and fellow SNCC organizers attempted to receive service at a Winona, Mississippi, bus station (Bracey, 2011; Young, 1996). Many whites in positions of power at the time did not take the beating of Hamer seriously or view it as out of the ordinary. White authority took precedence, and the cruelty exhibited by white men to uphold their dominant status in society was deemed justified (Bracey, 2011; Larson, 2021).

SNCC: Attempts to Register to Vote

One of the common threads between Fannie Lou Hamer and civil rights activists of her time were their efforts to protect, implement, and/or expand voting rights for Black people in the United States. In late August 1962, Hamer and seventeen other brave SNCC volunteers boarded an old bus to attempt to register to vote. The community-based leadership model of SNCC was attractive to Hamer, who wanted local autonomy in order to achieve political results (Lee, 1999: 23).[4] Student Nonviolent Coordinating Committee activists had, by and large, gotten their start during sit-ins across the US South.[5]

Hamer once said, "Don't go telling me anybody that ain't been in Mississippi two weeks and don't know nothing about the problem, because they're not leading us" (Bracey, 2011: 65). The SNCC strategy was to find local talent and extract the leadership qualities and knowledge they already possessed. This ultimate grassroots strategy was a ground-up approach, unlike, say, that of the National Association for the Advancement of Colored People (NAACP). The slow strategy of the NAACP, which waged legal battles throughout the courts at all levels, was a harder sell for those needing and demanding more immediate results.[6] The work of SNCC also highlighted the interplay between local, state, and national politics. By focusing on local politics within a system of larger national political struggles, SNCC exposed unjust southern state laws as a way to galvanize national support among Blacks and non-Blacks.

The right to vote remained an elusive tool for Black people seeking to control their own political and economic destinies. The ability to utilize the franchise would, in many ways, change the composition of leadership, empower Black people in policy arenas, and, more symbolically, include Black people as fuller citizens in American democracy. The vote was not only a tangible act of inclusion for Black citizens into the polity but also a symbol of hope. As Black people became empowered to exercise their full franchise under the law in the face of threats, beatings, abuse, and even death, those brave individuals moved the needle one step closer for the collective endeavor of electoral

---

[4] Much of this philosophy was rooted in Ella Baker's model of local empowerment. As one of the early organizers of SNCC and the 1964 Freedom Summer, designed to assist Black residents in Mississippi in their registration and voting efforts, Baker famously argued that "strong people don't need strong leaders" (Carson, 1981). Baker also ran a voter registration campaign called the Crusade for Citizenship.

[5] Young SNCC activists like John Lewis, James Bevel, Robert Moses, and James Forman were known for their brave sit-ins and the repercussions that followed (Bracey, 2011; Carson, 1981).

[6] Political historians by and large agree that the multipronged-strategy approach spread out across several organizations was beneficial on local and federal levels. The legal strategies of the NAACP and the more grassroots efforts of groups like SNCC, SCLC, and CORE (to name just a few) benefited the various strategies needed in cities and small towns across the United States.

inclusion (Chafe et al., 2011; Grant, 2020; Painter, 2021). Shortly after they assembled, Hamer and her SNCC comrades descended on the Indianola, Mississippi, courthouse to attempt to register to vote. The significance of Indianola stemmed from the fact that in 1960, Black people made up 60 percent of the voting-age population in Sunflower County, where Indianola resided, yet Black people made up only 1.2 percent of registered voters in that county (Larson, 2021; Lee, 1999).

To begin to understand the danger of this endeavor and the bravery of those involved, it is important to note that Indianola was the birthplace of the White Citizens' Council, a white supremacist group founded solely in response to *Brown* v. *Board of Education*, the landmark 1954 Supreme Court decision outlawing segregated schools (Blain, 2021; Lee, 1999). As Hamer answered the twenty-one questions that were part of the registration, she was keenly aware that providing answers to questions pertaining to her place of employment, her employer's name, and her place of residence placed her and her family in danger because this information would most certainly be turned over to the White Citizens' Council for them to share or retaliate as they saw fit.

As Chana Kai Lee outlines in *For Freedom's Sake: The Life of Fannie Lou Hamer*, the experience of traveling to the Indianola courthouse to attempt to register to vote left an indelible mark on Hamer and in many ways served as a catalytic moment that shifted Hamer's individual model of survival to an understanding of the power of collective organizing and shared struggle (Lee, 1999: 30). On their way home, the bus was stopped by local police who attempted to give the bus driver a fine of $100 because his bus was the wrong color (the officer argued that it looked too similar to a school bus). When neither the bus driver nor the group could produce the money, the officer attempted to arrest the bus driver on frivolous charges. Hamer and her SNCC comrades then decided that they should all be arrested to protect the bus driver, a man who was risking his own life and livelihood by driving them to register to vote. When the arresting officer realized that bringing in almost two dozen organized Black people who were attempting to register to vote could turn into a larger civil rights story and bring attention to him, his department, and the larger issue, he decided that he would be satisfied with a $30 fee to be paid on the spot. Hamer and the group pooled their money and avoided arrest, the confiscation of the bus, or worse. This experience moved Hamer from her previous mindset of survival and toward a new way of viewing her struggle through a collective lens. Hamer often spoke of this experience as instrumental in helping her truly see the power of the vote and why so many whites in Mississippi would go to great lengths to prevent Black people from mobilizing toward that effort. Not only was there safety in numbers, but relying on one's community could lead to advancement for the individual and the collective.

It is important to note the numerous risks associated with being a Black female grassroots organizer in the South (Bracey, 2011; Egerton, 1970). As Hamer became more involved in the voter registration process, the level of physical harassment and economic retaliation that she (and her family) experienced increased exponentially. When the white plantation owner demanded that Hamer rescind her request to register to vote, he gave her two options: go to the Indianola courthouse and withdraw her registration request or be fired and move off the property the next day. In addition to stipulating that Hamer leave the property if she refused to rescind her voter registration request, the plantation owner also demanded that her husband remain on the property to fulfill his financial obligations as a sharecropper on the land. Hamer did not need to wait until the following morning to give him an answer – she moved out that evening, leaving her family behind. Once Hamer had left her home, she stayed with various friends for two months. During this time, one of the homes in which she was staying was shot into sixteen times. No one was harmed, but Hamer (and her various gracious hosts) lived under the extreme threat of violence, prompting Hamer's move to Ruleville, Mississippi.

After participating in organizing via SNCC and workshops that assisted her in better understanding the need for a collective sense of determination as a citizen in the United States, Hamer recognized the indignity of so many being denied the right to vote for so long. As Hamer saw herself as an active member of and participant in the Civil Rights Movement, not only in Mississippi but also across the United States, a level of impatience grew within her for justice long denied – for herself as well as for countless other Black people who had been denied the franchise just as she had.

In January 1963, Hamer learned that she had passed the registration exam and would not need to try a third time. However, she did not have the requisite two poll-tax receipts required in Mississippi and other Black Belt states and was therefore unable to vote.[7] The taxes needed to be paid in consecutive years; therefore, Hamer was not able to cast her first vote until May 1964 (Larson, 2021; Lee, 1999). The common theme of Hamer as the simultaneous hero and victim was on full display once she successfully registered to vote. Indeed, Hamer served as a beacon of bravery for Black Mississippians who saw her

---

[7] The Black Belt consists of an eleven-state region originally labeled as such for the dark color of its soil and later for its high percentage of African American residents. There are more than 600 counties, stretching from southern Virginia to East Texas. The Black Belt eventually became the nation's largest contiguous pocket of poverty, high unemployment, poor education, declining population, and persistent health problems (Reeves, 2017).

efforts of advancing electoral participation as noble and ultimately beneficial to the entire community. However, per Mississippi law, the names of everyone who registered to vote were listed in the newspaper for a minimum of two weeks. Thus, Hamer's success in registering to vote brought unwanted attention by law enforcement and harassment by white vigilantes.[8]

Much of the motivation behind Hamer's drive to register her fellow Mississippians and the bravery she consistently displayed stemmed from her belief that Black people deserved to have their humanity and rights as citizens recognized. Most white Mississippians at this time fundamentally believed that Black people not only were not deserving of the full rights and privileges of full citizenship but were also somehow less than human, which justified their own cruel treatment of Black people on a daily basis in almost all facets of their lives. Supporting these beliefs were laws, power, and authoritarian figures who upheld the system of unfair and inhumane treatment. During this time in the US South, Mississippi was in the throes of complete Jim Crow rules and norms. It was unmistaken that Mississippi and other southern states were "authoritarian enclaves" refusing to embrace democratic practices or inclusion of Black citizens (Mickey, 2015).

In the 1960s, Mississippi was heralded as the most racist and oppressive state in the union. White domestic terrorism allowed the authoritarian system to exist within the state. The control by white Mississippians, oftentimes with brute force, severely limited organizing efforts within the state. Black people feared economic retaliation, brutal force, and even death (Bracey, 2011; Stoper, 1977). Hamer's introduction to the young SNCC activists at a local Black church in Ruleville significantly shifted her outlook on the movement, her role as a leader in the movement, and the larger mission of Black liberation (and democracy). Part of Hamer's success was her attention to detail (something her employers on plantations had always highlighted), as well as her ability to connect and relate to people no matter their circumstance (Blain, 2021; Larson, 2021).

Although Hamer was successful in registering thousands of Mississippians across the state in the early 1960s, she and her SNCC comrades did face difficulties when organizing. Some Black people felt that risking their lives and livelihoods for the right to vote was more than they could endure (Blain,

---

[8] Hamer and her comrades endured white vigilantes entering their homes with guns and flashlights in the middle of the night. On one occasion, the Ruleville sheriff, S. L. Milam, accompanied the white vigilantes on their harassment mission. To contextualize the constant threat of danger for the Hamers, Sheriff Milam was the brother of J. W. Milam, one of the accused murderers of Emmett Till, the fourteen-year-old Chicago boy brutally tortured and murdered for allegedly whistling at a white girl. Till's death became a pivotal moment in the Civil Rights Movement when his mother, Mamie Till, chose to have an open-casket funeral so the world would see what white supremacists in the South had done to her child.

2021; Larson, 2021). Others felt that they had already been through enough without further risking their futures. And another portion of Black people had reached tacit agreements with whites in exchange for their abstaining from organizing efforts (Bracey, 2011). Whites relied on violence, or the threat of violence, to maintain dominance and control over Black people within the state and the southern region more broadly. Violence as an intimidation technique was a powerful and useful tool used to deprive Black people of their constitutional rights at the ballot booth and beyond (Williams, 1987). Whites in power were determined to maintain this social order by any means necessary. Therefore, it was Hamer's job to convince Black Mississippians to join the political struggle and convince them that despite the real threat of violence and loss of livelihood, the larger democratic project was more important for their lives and the lives of their descendants. As Hamer explained why she was tired of being oppressed, she advocated for civil disobedience as a means to begin to change what was a calcified and inequitable system of white political dominance over Black citizens (Bracey, 2011; Williams, 1987). What many whites understood was that control of Black people on the local level, electorally and economically, could dictate state-level policies and in turn continue to set precedents at the national level.

As E. N. Bracey (2011) argues in *Fannie Lou Hamer: The Life of a Civil Rights Icon*, in the summer of 1964, often referred to as Freedom Summer, the registration efforts in Mississippi reached a boiling point. Before the summer of 1964, there was no real coordinated effort in the Black community toward a robust Civil Rights Movement in Mississippi. The danger Black Mississippians experienced was often described as horrifying and unmatched on a global scale. The violence inflicted on Black people and their communities ranged from arrests and beatings to shootings, bombings, and death.[9] Hamer and her fellow SNCC organizers knew that in order for her efforts to be successful and for Black people to begin a political path toward inclusion and equality, they would need to reach Black Mississippians in all parts of the state and from all walks of life, thus recognizing the importance of local and state political practices as harbingers of potential national policy changes. Historically, white Mississippians had done everything in their power to prevent Black Mississippians from voting.[10] People like Fannie Lou Hamer – poor, with

---

[9] During the violent summer of 1964 in Mississippi, Black activist James Chaney and white activists Andrew Goodman and Michael Schwerner were found murdered. Once the press highlighted the deaths, white sympathy for the movement began to increase. However, the violence that Black people endured included thousands of arrests, with thirty-five people shot, eighty beatings, thirty buildings bombed, and three people killed (Hine and Thompson, 1999).

[10] Student Nonviolent Coordinating Committee members and their allies may have been dedicated to nonviolence, but many white southerners were not. It was not uncommon for white

limited education, and reliant on sharecropping for economic stability – were often directly targeted for disenfranchisement and political exclusion. However, Hamer felt that it was her duty to educate Black people about their constitutional rights. It was during this summer that Hamer decided to devote her life to the goal of Black liberation.

Mississippi Freedom Democratic Party

The crux of so much of Hamer's organizing is the interplay between local, state, and national politics and policy. A key element of the strategy of Hamer and her colleagues was organizing on the local level in order to change state-level policies while also bringing attention to unjust practices and policies on a national level. Hamer was a grassroots organizer who focused on expanding the franchise for Black Americans and marginalized people across the US South. Through her work with SNCC, she helped build an infrastructure to expand the project of democracy on local and state levels in order to influence national politics. As a Black woman who relied on the efforts of other local organizers in states across the US South to help improve national conditions, Hamer built power bases outside of traditional party structures. For Hamer, this was made possible through the creation of the MFDP.

Hamer survived the registration efforts of the summer of 1964 and focused on building political power outside of the all-white Democratic Party in Mississippi. Hamer also began to teach citizenship classes to help her fellow Mississippians better understand how all elements of the political process affected their lives (Bracey, 2011: 84). As a result, Hamer was away from her family and community for long stretches of time, speaking at meetings across the state and fundraising throughout the country. These efforts had the specific aim to raise awareness of the economic and political injustices and violence occurring in Mississippi, as well as generate national support for the plight of Black people in hopes of federal intervention (Asch, 2008: 209; Bracey, 2011: 91).

The work of Black-led organizations is crucial to our understanding of how and why these organizations do the work. The previous failures by organizations to advance causes pertaining to Black freedom and justice necessitated the emergence of new grassroots organizations and even political parties. The MFDP was a multiracial coalition formed to challenge the all-too-powerful and authoritarian all-white Democratic Party in Mississippi and was also made up of mostly rural Black Mississippians with little to no political experience

---

southerners to use bottles, rocks, bricks, and bombs to attack Black people in broad daylight without fear of retribution or state-sanctioned punishment (Rubel, 1990).

(Bracey, 2011). The party officially took shape on April 26, 1964, during a rally of 200 people at the state capitol in Jackson (Ransby, 2003). To achieve the goal of Black participation in the electoral process, Hamer and other MFDP founders hoped the formation of this new party would allow for maximum participation of Black people in the political process by giving them an alternative to the racist Mississippi Democratic Party. When Hamer attended a precinct meeting of the Democratic Party in Ruleville, which was characteristically all white, her participation was not welcomed or permitted (Ransby, 2003). Her presence was also interpreted as a threat to the white power structure and the political status quo. That meeting made it abundantly clear to Hamer that integration into the Democratic Party would not be welcomed or accepted and that the only recourse was to establish a separate political party open to an integrated and multiracial vision of political equity (Bracey, 2011). Hamer's political aspiration to create something more inclusive of and specific to the Black electoral and democratic project is rooted in her work with the MFDP. Hamer had a desire to build a foundation and no longer accept the scraps given by the Democratic Party. Her work within the MFDP was part of her broader goal to build a democratic institution that recognized and supported Black political participation.

Hamer's recognition of the limitations of the traditional two-party system led her to establish a party separate from the established power structure. Her political imagination was born from her myriad experiences as a Black woman seeking equality at the ballot box and in society writ large. The de jure racism of the American South at the time was what bell hooks (2004) has described as the interplay of white supremacy, anti-Black racism, racialized capitalism, and patriarchy. Hamer understood that in order to begin to dismantle these forces and hold America to account for not living up to its democratic ideals, she would need to organize on grassroots levels to help others understand the possibility and promise of the democratic project. Working with other Black leaders, and Black women in particular, Hamer was able to focus her efforts away from the Democratic Party and toward organizing Black southerners on building a party that was of, led by, and for Black people. Hamer's efforts were rooted in the belief that America has the capacity to change, to evolve, and to ultimately move closer to her stated promises.

The MFDP "was developed for three basic reasons: (1) the long history of systemic exclusion of black citizen from equal participation in the political process in the state, (2) because the Mississippi Democratic Party had conclusively demonstrated its lack of loyalty to the National Democratic Party; and (3) the determination of the state's 'power structure' to maintain the status quo" (McLemore, 1971). The significance of the MFDP stemmed from the sheer audacity of the formation of a new political party to challenge and extricate some of the carte blanche power of the established all-white Democratic Party. The Mississippi Democratic Party further exposed its white-supremacist roots and inclinations when it adopted a platform opposing civil rights and rejecting the national party platform (Williams, 1987). Since the Mississippi Democratic Party was out of step with the national party platform, the MFDP hoped it would be able to gain recognition as the official delegation from Mississippi and gain exclusive delegate representation at the DNC in Atlantic City in August 1964 (Dittmer, 1994).

In addition to attempts at unseating the established, all-white Mississippi Democratic Party, Hamer and her fellow organizers hoped to raise awareness of the plight of Black people in Mississippi and engage in a national conversation about race and the ballot while at the convention. In preparation for the DNC, members of the MFDP established offices in Washington, DC, months before-hand in order to organize and educate northerners about the treatment of Black people in the political sphere and the incredibly violent and white-supremacist political system in Mississippi (Bracey, 2011). The work of political education for Black people, in the north *and* south, was a necessary strategy if Hamer and her fellow organizers were to lay a lasting foundation of democracy building. Throughout the spring and summer of 1964, thousands of Black Mississippians joined the MFDP, an organization with vocal and visible female leadership.[11]

Much of the pre-DNC organizing was spearheaded by Ella Baker, who arranged logistics and served as a mentor to many in the Mississippi delegation. Baker was fiercely loyal to Hamer and supported her efforts as a burgeoning organizer and assisted her in better understanding the political ramifications of challenging the all-white Mississippi Democratic Party. Baker's efforts laid the foundation for Hamer to circumvent white politicians' attempts to silence her and her fellow MFDP members. Although Baker began as the head of the MFDP, Hamer replaced her as the voice of the Mississippi movement. Baker provided steadfast support to the MFDP, and to Hamer more specifically, and continued to share her expertise and political strategies with Hamer and the other members of the MFDP leading up to and through the 1964 convention.[12]

White Democratic leaders did not want to allow Hamer to describe in detail the ways that Black citizens in Mississippi were being denied the franchise and the full benefits of American democracy, as well as the injustices and oppression that she and so many others suffered. Those details would be too embarrassing on a national and international scale. Therefore, there were widespread efforts to make sure the

---

[11] Other MFDP organizers included Annie Devine and Victoria Gray (Ransby, 2003). For a more detailed account of the other Black women who laid much of the foundation for organizing and coalition building during the Civil Rights Movement, see Ransby (2003).

[12] These Black female coalitions served as blueprints for Black female leadership in the South seen fifty-plus years later with Stacey Abrams and in the efforts of female organizers like LaTosha Brown, Nsé Ufot, and Helen Butler.

MFDP did not gain a national audience at the 1964 DNC (Blain, 2021; Larson, 2021). Recognizing the newly emerging national Civil Rights Movement, Hamer and SNCC altered their strategies and political perspective by affirming Black self-determination and challenged their white northern allies to take a stronger stance in support of the Black southern movements. In doing so, SNCC empowered and emboldened oppressed Black people in Mississippi to have and control their own independent political organization.[13] The sheer number of Black people living in the US South without the full franchise was a keen reminder of the geographic limitations placed on Black citizens in Mississippi and neighboring southern states. As national Democratic Party politicians slowly began the process of incorporating Black Americans into party politics, and northern cities began courting Black voters and electing Black candidates for local and state-level offices, the abundant electoral oppression in the US South served as a stain and a clear reminder of democracy unfulfilled.

Not only did whites in Mississippi not believe that Hamer and other MFDP members were capable of political strategies but they also resented the group for trying to amass political power throughout the state. What made the MFDP even more insidious in the eyes of many white Mississippians were the efforts to find economic commonalities between both races in order to advance the political futures of Black people and whites in the state. The goal of the MFDP was not only to organize political advancement but also to educate potential voters, both Black and white (Bracey, 2011).

The formation of the MFDP served as a catalytic moment for Black Mississippians. They were empowered to envision a society and political process that did not exclude and oppress them. The year 1964 brought Freedom Summer volunteers to Mississippi to work alongside Hamer and her comrades, and not only did they register Black Mississippians but they also showed them what their political lives could be. The MFDP eventually registered close to 80,000 people in its Freedom Ballot campaign (Hine and Thompson, 1999).[14] With the assistance of SNCC and CORE volunteers,[15] young Black people were especially motivated

---

[13] Similar to the African independence movements occurring at the time, one of the goals of the MFDP was to allow Black people in Mississippi to emancipate themselves from the pro-segregationist Democratic Party (Ransby, 2003).

[14] The Freedom Ballot initiative was that under the MFDP, Fannie Lou Hamer and colleagues ran for Congress on an alternative ballot, separate from the official Democratic Party ballot. This unofficial ballot was not ultimately recognized by the state of Mississippi as valid, and therefore, the success of Hamer on the Freedom Ballot did not change the listings of candidate names on the official Democratic Party ballot. However, Hamer received significantly more votes on the Freedom Ballot than her white Democratic Party opponent, Congressman Jamie Whitten, proving that Hamer was a leader who was capable of defeating a white opponent (Reed, 1993).

[15] The Congress of Racial Equality, or CORE, was founded in 1942 by an interracial group of students in Chicago.

to try to cast their lot with a new political party. Although they were young, their frustration with being denied the full franchise simmered, and the summer of 1964 gave them an organizing outlet to make their political dreams a more concrete reality (Ransby, 2003). However, arrival at the DNC in Atlantic City presented several challenges to the newly organized members of the MFDP.[16]

The most egregious anti-MFDP act came from President Lyndon B. Johnson.[17] Johnson was intent on silencing Hamer and her harrowing account of the political conditions in Mississippi, and on stopping her attempts to register Black Mississippians to vote. As the DNC raged on, white southern Democrats came to view Johnson as a race traitor and a traitor to the South. As LBJ desperately tried to regain control of an orchestrated convention, his party, and the narrative, he had to contend with those from within his own party, and from his region, who opposed civil rights and had no intention of supporting the national Democratic ticket. He feared that if he acknowledged and supported the efforts of the MFDP, he would lose other Southern delegates, not just from Mississippi but from other states as well. His fear that these delegates would walk out of the convention in protest were real enough for him to first try to deflect attention from the MFDP's efforts by calling an emergency and impromptu faux news conference[18] to be aired at the same time as Hamer's DNC speech. Johnson needed to divert the focus away from Hamer in order to protect his own coalitions and electoral ambitions (Ransby, 2003). Ultimately, LBJ sent Hubert Humphrey to negotiate with the MFDP. In an attempt to reach a "compromise," the MFDP was allotted symbolic seats on the convention floor alongside the all-white Democratic Party, a gesture that Hamer rejected outright. Hamer's examination of the state-level

---

[16] Hamer and her comrades initially went to the 1964 DNC filled with a sense of hope and optimism pertaining to the capacity for change within the Democratic Party. "When we went to Atlantic City, we went there because we believed that America was what it said it was, 'the land of the free.' And I thought with all of my heart that the [white] people would have been unseated in Atlantic City. And I believed that, because if the Constitution of this United States means something to all of us, then I knew they would unseat them. So we went to Atlantic City with all of this hope" (Bracey, 2011: 110).

[17] LBJ was a complex figure within the civil rights struggle. The same president who worked tirelessly to silence Fannie Lou Hamer and the MFDP, LBJ also mentored Barbara Jordan and helped usher the passage of the Civil Rights Act in 1964 and the Voting Rights Act and the Immigration Act of 1965 (Greer, 2018b).

[18] Johnson's famous press conference to deflect from the powerful testimony of Fannie Lou Hamer as the representative of the MFDP will forever politically link LBJ and Hamer. As Hamer began to recount the harrowing details of her beating in Winona, Mississippi, Johnson hastily convened members of the press at the White House with thirty Democratic governors. This ruse made the press believe that Johnson would be announcing his vice presidential choice. However, Johnson stalled during the meeting without announcing his vice presidential pick or any news of consequence (Bracey, 2011). Poet and essayist June Jordan (1972) believed that when American people "heard [Hamer] speak, all good people were shocked by her suffering." And when all was said and done, "[t]housands and thousands of people wanted to help her [Hamer] on to a freedom victory."

exclusionary practices played out on a national level. This understanding further contributed to a growing movement of Black people who wanted increased electoral inclusion in their respective home states as well as on the national level. Many people are familiar with the now iconic photo of Hamer speaking about the inequities and brutality she and her fellow Black southerners faced. Sitting with microphones in front of her, she detailed the atrocities occurring in Mississippi and across the US South for the nation (and the world) to hear.

Hamer will forever be known for two achievements. First, she developed organizations with the sole goal of and focus on securing the vote. She transformed some of the calcified structures used to oppress Black people by using inside and outside tactics. She used local and state-level political inequities in Mississippi to garner national attention and instigate change within the national Democratic Party. The second permanent contribution of Hamer and her legacy is how she changed the way Black people saw themselves. She was a woman from humble beginnings, a sharecropper with limited education, whose belief in herself and her people led her to influence presidential politics. Hamer was a symbol for Black people, for women, for poor people, and for Black women in particular. There were no internal limits for Hamer. Her steadfast faith and belief that Black people should and could be free shone like a light. She was undeterred and changed the course of southern politics. Her coalition-building efforts on behalf of Black people served as a blueprint for the likes of Stacey Abrams almost half a century later.

3 Barbara Jordan: The Lone Star

Firsts are often celebrated, and those who came before them are often mere footnotes to the larger narrative. Shirley Chisholm (D-NY) became the first Black woman elected to the US House of Representatives in 1968. As the first Black woman in Congress, Chisholm was known as a trailblazer and firebrand, challenging racial and gender norms while in office. Four years after her historic win, Barbara Jordan was elected as the second Black woman ever to serve in Congress. However, in 1972, Jordan was a first in her own right as the first Black woman elected to Congress from the US South.[19]

---

[19] During the 1972 election, Yvonne Brathwaite Burke was also elected to the House of Representatives from California. In January 1973, when Jordan and Burke were both sworn in, the largest number of African Americans were serving in Congress since Reconstruction. A total of fifteen Black American members of the House and Edward Brooke, the African American Republican senator from Massachusetts, made up the largest and most geographically diverse group of Black congresspeople in the history of the United States (Rogers, 1998: 176). Burke is not celebrated or studied as much as Barbara Jordan, even though Burke left Congress at

Malcolm X aptly stated, "When we say South, we mean south of the Canadian border. America in its entirety is segregationist and is racist. It's more camouflaged in the north, but it's the same thing."[20] Essentially, Malcolm X argued that there was little daylight between the racist practices and inequities in the North and those in the South. However, in the mid-twentieth century, there were still blatant distinctions between northern and southern opportunities. Therefore, the election of Chisholm from New York and then the election of Jordan from Texas, a solidly southern state, did mark an achievement for a Black woman from the Fifth Ward of Houston. When Jordan returned to Texas from Boston University School of Law, no white law firm would hire her. Thus, she began her own law practice while sitting at her parents' kitchen table. Jordan was raised in a civic-minded family that believed not only in personal advancement but also in group uplift. With a foundation from her grandparents, Jordan's interest in public service began to bloom. After practicing law in Texas for a few years, she ran unsuccessfully for the Texas Legislature in 1962 and 1964. Those initial setbacks were real but not insurmountable.

This section will explore the life and political legacy of the first Black woman elected to the House of Representatives from the US South. Jordan set an example for Black women in electoral politics at the state and federal levels that enabled them and other future Black elected officials to see themselves as orators, policymakers, change agents, and occasional autonomous leaders in the fight for civil rights and increased enfranchisement of marginalized groups in the United States. I detail the life and legacy of Barbara Jordan and her transformational Democratic leadership and interracial coalition building to help readers better understand the democratic path in US politics, as well as Jordan's efforts to increase the number of participants in the electorate more broadly.

Jordan's contributions to electoral politics helped lay the foundation for the myriad Black women who have subsequently been elected to statehouses and congressional seats across the country in the last fifty years. Several political scientists have chronicled the contributions of Black women in electoral politics (Brown, 2014; Brown and Gershon, 2016; Simien, 2006; Smooth, 2011), and social scientists have analyzed the significance of the South in our understanding of American political development and the ebbs and flows of democratic practices in the United States (Chafe et al., 2011; Painter, 2021).

---

the same time as Jordan after three terms and had a long career at varying levels of California politics.

[20] Ballot or the Bullet speech, www.newstatesman.com/world-affairs/2013/04/when-ns-met-malcolm-x.

As a southerner and the first Black woman from the US South to serve as an elected official in Congress – unlike Hamer, who organized Black people across the South – Jordan chose to make her contribution to strengthening American democracy through formal political means, working her way into the institutions of the Texas statehouse and US Congress. Working within formal political structures presented a different set of challenges as she attempted to change calcified electoral structures. Formal politics also presented opportunities to build coalitions.

The Texas Political Landscape

Jordan was not initially successful in her races for the Texas Legislature. She later discovered that those who knew and supported her were not being represented equally. Their ballots were being diluted by the votes of those who did not know her and/or those who would not vote for a Black woman. Jordan realized she was playing by the rules, but the deck was stacked against her. At this time, legislative districts were malapportioned, gerrymandered, and not representative of constituents who actually resided in them. In 1960s Texas, attempts to provide citizens with racial or gender representation were relatively nonexistent. Jordan knew that the gerrymandered composition of the Texas districts would never yield qualified candidates like herself.

Two landmark Supreme Court cases changed the electoral fate of Jordan and likely many other candidates across the country. In the 1962 case *Baker* v. *Carr*, the high court ruled that legislative reapportionment was an issue to be decided by the courts. In the 1964 case *Reynolds* v. *Sims*, it ruled that districts in both houses of a bicameral legislature must be of equal proportion. Then, in 1965, a three-judge federal court case, *Kilgarlin* v. *Martin*, ordered the Texas Legislature to redraw House and Senate districts to reflect the new "one person, one vote" rule. The court also struck down two provisions of the Texas Constitution: The first one limited a county to one state senator, and the other provision prevented any county from having more than seven members in the Texas House of Representatives. The Texas Legislature did reapportion, which helped lead to the election of Jordan to the Texas State Senate in 1966 (Sherman, 2007: 51–52).

Jordan's election to the Texas Senate in 1966 was the first for an African American woman in the state.[21] In addition, Jordan's electoral victory in Texas

---

[21] Grace Towns Hamilton was elected to the Georgia House of Representatives in 1965 and took office in 1966, becoming *the* first Black woman in the US South to hold elected office in a statehouse (Spritzer and Bergmark, 2009).

was the first for an African American since 1883, during the Reconstruction period.[22] Jordan's understanding of the legislative process and her exceptional oratorical skills were so effective that her thirty white male colleagues named her outstanding freshman senator during her first year in office (Sherman, 2007: 80–81). Some of Jordan's signature legislation during her six years in the Texas State Senate pertained to creating the Fair Employment Practices Commission and providing for its regulation of discriminatory acts in employment (S.B. 79), requiring contracting agencies in various political subcultures in the state to include nondiscriminatory provisions (S.B. 81), restructuring permits for construction of public housing on urban-renewal land (S.B. 82), and providing a duty-free lunch period for teachers without lengthening the school day (S.B. 83), to name a few.

Jordan's effectiveness as a legislator had rippling effects for working-class laborers in Texas. Laundry workers, domestic workers, and farm laborers were just some of the groups aided by Jordan's legislative efforts. During her tenure in the Texas statehouse, Jordan also authored legislation pertaining to workers' compensation in certain districts (S.B. 264 and S.B. 265), establishing a Department of Labor within the state (S.B. 289), and creating an Urban Assistance Board (S.B. 384). Almost half of the bills she proposed while working as a state senator in Austin were enacted into law (Sherman, 2007: 92) and were aimed at assisting the working class and poor in Texas (Sherman, 2007: 92).[23] There she took up the cause of the working poor because for them, like so many other Americans, and African Americans in particular, poverty or the possibility of it loomed large. This desire to help working-class Black Texans served as a foundation for her willingness to work with others.

Jordan pushed through legislation that gave the state its first minimum-wage law, an accomplishment that the liberal *Texas Observer* hailed as "a near miracle" (Rogers, 1998: 146) and was instrumental in erecting the Texas Fair Employment Commission (Berry and Gross, 2020: 199). Jordan understood that in order for the policies for which she fought tirelessly to actually assist her Houston constituents, they would need both a minimum wage and a commission to further protect their employment. Jordan was also able to convince some of her colleagues who represented other urban and even rural areas of Texas to support legislation that could benefit a great number of Texans, not just the Black constituents in Jordan's district (Donaldson, 2017; Rogers, 1998).

---

[22] The Reconstruction period that followed the Civil War was marked by both progress and regression for Black Americans in the political sphere from the mid-1860s through the 1920s.

[23] Similar to when Shirley Chisholm served in the New York State Assembly and helped write legislation pertaining to child care, education, women's rights, and more.

Jordan's rise to political power at the state level contributed to a confluence of events that shaped not only her own career but also her political presence, which had rippling effects at the highest levels of power and national politics. As mandated in the US Constitution, a census of the population must be conducted every ten years to take stock of the population. The Texas legislative session in 1971 immediately followed the 1970 census, which mandated that the Texas Legislature reapportion its state and federal districts to account for population changes. Because of the need to redraw districts, a safe Democratic political district was drawn in the heart of Houston, and in 1972, Jordan was elected with 80 percent of the total vote and 90 percent of the Black vote (Rogers, 1998; Sherman, 2007).

Jordan in Congress

During this same election of 1972, in which Jordan was elected to represent the state of Texas in the halls of Congress, Richard Nixon was reelected as the thirty-seventh president of the United States when he defeated George McGovern by winning forty-nine states and garnering 61 percent of the popular vote. Many scholars often link Jordan to former president Lyndon Johnson due to their Texas roots and his mentorship during her tenure in Congress. However, the career of Jordan is inextricably linked to that of Nixon because of Jordan's role as a junior member of the House Judiciary Committee. Jordan's unwavering belief in the potential of America to change for the better and live up to its democratic ideals led her to become a leader in the efforts to uphold the promise of American democracy, even if it meant holding a US president accountable.

When Jordan arrived in Washington, DC, she came with a certain level of "protection" due to her connections with Johnson. The former president firmly believed that had it not been for the constraints of Jordan's race and sex, she could have been president of the United States.[24] His willingness to assist Jordan in her success as a junior legislator made Jordan a powerful force in the halls of the Capitol. It also created tensions for Jordan with her colleagues in the CBC when her ambitions and agenda did not fully align with that of the larger group of mostly male and mostly northern legislators. In 1972, the majority of Black Americans lived in the South and experienced a different type of racism, with Jim Crow and electoral disenfranchisement, from that experienced by their Black counterparts in northern cities. However, the vast

---

[24] Jordan, while reflecting on what Johnson meant to her at the Great Society Roundup in 1990, said, "Lyndon Johnson made me believe I could be president of the United States . . . I believed it because he believed it. Can you imagine what such faith does for one's self-concept? No limits. Free to soar. A level playing field. No artificial barriers. He was saying to me, believe in yourself, as I believe in you" (Rogers, 1998: 175).

majority of Black electoral representation hailed from northern urban centers. Hence, there was a troubled disconnect between masses of Black American citizens and their representation by Black members in Congress (Rogers, 1998). Part of the tension and disconnect between Jordan as a southerner and her colleagues stemmed from the fact that the majority of her CBC colleagues represented northern and midwestern urban centers, and Jordan and Andrew Young (D-GA) were the only two congressional representatives elected from the US South. Although the majority of Black people resided in southern states, descriptive representation on the Congressional level did not reflect the numbers of Black citizens residing in districts in the South. Due to varying forms of gerrymandering in northern districts, Black representation on the Congressional level was more significant in northern locales. Johnson was a powerful ally to Jordan, which led her CBC colleagues to tacitly tolerate certain choices that she made. Similarly to Jordan, Stacey Abrams negotiated and worked alongside more conservative colleagues in order to pass (or block) legislation, occasionally creating tensions with other Black colleagues in the statehouse and local officials who differed in their coalition-building approaches.

When Jordan arrived in Congress and was placed on the committee, she was ranked thirty-eighth on a thirty-eight-member committee. During her first year and a half in Congress, Jordan acclimated herself to the inner workings of the federal-level legislative process. In 1974, it was revealed that President Nixon had possibly betrayed the trust of the American people and divorced himself from the principles stated in the US Constitution, and the House of Representatives began to organize itself for possible impeachment proceedings. During the disclosure process, vast cover-ups by Nixon and his administration were exposed, and Jordan emerged as a strong voice amid national political turmoil, and a stalwart defender of democracy. As a member of the Judiciary Committee, Jordan displayed a clear-eyed understanding of constitutional limits and a respect for the legal process for all the nation to see.

On July 24, 1974, Jordan delivered her landmark speech during Nixon's impeachment hearings. She laid out the president's actions and why they posed a threat to the United States and to the Constitution. Jordan used her fifteen minutes on national television to articulate the dangers of Nixon's actions to the democratic republic and related these remarks to her personal experience as a Black American woman.[25] Jordan's address to the nation clearly

---

[25] An excerpt of Jordan's speech was thus: "My faith in the Constitution is whole, it is complete, it is total. I am not going to sit here and be an idle spectator to the diminution, the subversion, the destruction of the Constitution . . . 'We the People' – it is a very eloquent beginning. But when the Constitution of the United States was completed on the seventeenth of September 1787, I was not included in that. 'We the People.' I felt for many years that somehow George Washington and

laid out the reasons why the country's elected officials must do what was in the best interests of the American people and impeach the sitting president (Berry and Gross, 2020: 199).

The importance of Barbara Jordan on a national scale cannot be overstated. The role of a member of US Congress is not only to represent their respective state but also to uphold the laws of the federal government. The important visual of Jordan, a Black woman, holding the president of the United States to account is one that many could not forget. Not only was Jordan on display for her colleagues and the world to see but also she approached this important moment with a level of eloquence and legal acumen that impressed her Democratic colleagues, frustrated her Republican colleagues, infuriated racists and segregationists, and ushered in a new level of understanding of the role Jordan would further play not just in the Nixon hearings but also within the Democratic Party more broadly.

Jordan's experience in the Texas statehouse no doubt prepared her for some of the racial, gender, and intraparty dynamics she would face in Washington, DC. As the first Black woman in Congress representing the US South, Jordan was able to integrate her grassroots experiences in Texas, her legal background, and her understanding of the interplay of race and immigration in order to work on behalf of Texans, Black people, and women. During her tenure, many of her contributions were behind the scenes, building coalitions between seemingly different members of Congress. Jordan's ability to work with CBC members, members of the Texas delegation, southern representatives, and even members of the opposing party were the key to her success in Congress. Jordan cosponsored diverse legislation pertaining to upholding the tax code, increasing Black representation at the Smithsonian Institution, extending the ratification of Equal Rights Amendment, and increasing housing for young families. Jordan's desire to promote and pass legislation also led her to establish alliances with other members of Congress that may have appeared uneasy or even peculiar to some.

The Voting Rights Act of 1975

I reject the hypothesis that our civil liberties may be either strictly observed or blatantly ignored depending on the whim of government officials. – Jordan (1976)[26]

Jordan fundamentally believed in the power of elected officials and electoral politics to transform the lives of Americans. She had seen how her grandfather

---

Alexander Hamilton just left me out by mistake. But through the process of amendment, interpretation, and court decision I have finally been included in 'We the People'" (Sherman, 2007).

[26] "Barbara Jordan Reports to the People of the 18th Congressional District of Texas" (newsletter), February 1976, Houston Public Library (Rogers, 1998: 247).

was able to purchase his modest home in Houston with assistance from the Home Finance Corporation, a program that expanded after the New Deal era. Both Franklin D. Roosevelt and Jordan's mentor Lyndon B. Johnson used money to change the lives of some of the poorest Americans and those who had been explicitly left out of the American Dream. She saw how effective use of elected officials' powers and national policies could affect everything from roads to schools to homes to rivers to the overall environment, changing the trajectory of one's life with the passage of legislation ... or its refusal. Jordan believed that the most efficient way for Americans to receive proper goods, services, and representation was to extend the franchise as inclusively and holistically as possible. Jordan believed that the fruits of democracy belonged in the hands of Americans who needed it most, not those who would add it to their already abundant supply of goods (Sherman, 2007). Because of this, Jordan worked to build coalitions with a broad swath of colleagues within Texas, across the South, among her CBC colleagues, and throughout the Democratic Party. Jordan's ties with Texan and other southern Democrats gave her the ability to influence dozens of legislators in ways that her fellow CBC members could not, and in ways that many of her white colleagues could not, either (Rogers, 1998).[27] In these instances, Jordan used her regional identity as her primary identity. Indeed, many of her colleagues felt more comfortable negotiating with other men; however, Jordan was not a northern Democrat representing northern big cities, and when necessary, she relied on the shared identity of being a Texan and/or a southerner to usher necessary legislation to fruition.

Before Jordan arrived in Washington, DC, her political mentor LBJ had signed the Civil Rights Act in 1964 and both the VRA and the Immigration and Nationality Act into law in 1965. The VRA of 1965 was important for two key reasons. First, it abolished the use of literacy tests, which seven southern states still used to disenfranchise Black people from the electoral process (Rogers, 1998). Second, the law assisted Black people, especially those in the South, in registering to vote without interference, in that the VRA gave the US

---

[27] The Congressional Black Caucus was founded in 1971 by thirteen Black American representatives in Congress. The caucus was formed to serve as a voice for the "national black community" after Dr. Martin Luther King, Jr.'s death. No singular Black leader emerged in the wake of King's death in 1968, and the caucus was formed to articulate policy platforms pertaining to education, health, racism, Africa, and so on. The caucus was initially not recognized by President Nixon, thus leading the CBC members to boycott Nixon's State of the Union address. Jordan believed that the primary role of the CBC should be legislative. Jordan stated, "I have told my Black Caucus colleagues that we cannot try to be the Urban League, the NAACP, the Urban Coalition, the Afro-Americans for Black Unity all rolled into one. We have a commonality of issue – blackness – but we cannot do what the other organizations have been designed to do through the years" (Rogers, 1998: 177; Sanders, 1975).

Justice Department and the attorney general discretionary power to appoint federal officials as "voting examiners." After the passage of the act, the increasing numbers of Black voters in the electoral sphere was met with structural changes by whites on an institutional level. The use of gerrymandered districts, consolidation of voting districts, and at-large elections were just some of the tools whites used to dilute the power of the Black vote and change the outcome of elections (Rogers, 1998).

Ten years later, in the summer of 1975, the VRA was up for renewal. Legislators, including CBC members, were organizing themselves for the extension of this important act, yet Jordan had her sights on something far more substantive: the *expansion* of the act. Jordan understood that the passage of the VRA allowed Black Americans to get one step closer to full inclusion and the full electoral rights and privileges of US citizens under the law, especially those from the South. Like Hamer, Jordan possessed an outsized vision of what American democracy could be. As Hamer worked with organizers to expand voting rights for Black people in the South, Jordan worked in Washington, DC, to help expand voting rights legislation that would secure basic democratic principles and policies for Black people. Through the interplay between insider and outsider tactics, coupled with northern and southern strategies, we see the ways that Hamer and Jordan advanced the foundation of democracy on local, statewide, and national levels. Both understood how profoundly federal policy would affect local and state actions. However, both were also keenly aware of how important local and state politics and organizing, of both ideas and ideals, were in order to influence national policy.

Despite the efforts of Hamer and Jordan, many southern states attempted to circumvent new federal civil right laws, and they were aided by national politicians. For example, during the passage of the 1965 VRA, President Johnson deliberately left Texas out of the legislation as part of a strategic effort to placate his white Texas colleagues and allies (Rogers, 1998). A decade later, as Jordan worked to extend the VRA, she quickly realized that the exclusion of Texas in the original bill was a glaring indication of the persistent exclusionary practices. The reluctance of Texas representatives on the state and federal levels to address voting discrimination against members of "language minority groups" slowed down the realization of democracy in the state. Jordan knew that Texas politicians would be reluctant to agree to end gerrymandering and at-large districts or submitting changes pertaining to election law to the Justice Department. It was these same practices that had kept Jordan out of political office over a decade prior. However, Jordan's efforts to extend the VRA did not sit well with her Texas colleagues who opposed Texas's inclusion in the federal law.[28] This tension between state and federal laws has existed since the country's inception. How states deal with inclusion and expansion in contrast with the federal government has been a contentious interplay between legislation and the courts for hundreds of years. Political differences and occasional minefields on the state and federal levels were a persistent presence for Jordan during her tenure in Congress, which she adeptly negotiated on a consistent basis. In the end, the passage of the VRA of 1975 included amendments that allowed for delayed expiration of certain provisions, geographic expansion that included Texas, and mandatory bilingual elections in certain areas. With the inclusion of language minorities as well as racial minorities, the 1975 amendments increased protections for Mexican Americans and Black people in Texas.

One of the many highlights of Jordan's career in Congress was the successful effort to expand the VRA to include language minorities in 1975. Jordan knew that if the VRA expired, the US South would most likely revert to its old ways of voter suppression toward Black people. She had come to the conclusion as a constitutional scholar that the Fifteenth Amendment – the 1870 amendment granting Black men the right to vote – also applied to non-Black people, more specifically, Spanish-speaking voters.[29] Because of this, Jordan felt it imperative to include provisions that allowed for bilingual ballots.[30] Jordan knew that expanding the franchise to include Mexican Americans in the amended 1975 VRA would move the nation closer to equity for all citizens in Texas, not just non-Hispanic Black and white citizens. The progress of the previous ten years would in essence disappear for millions of voters if the VRA of 1975 was not adequately updated and extended. With the 1980 decennial census on the horizon, Jordan knew well that the reapportionment of new districts would further dilute the Black vote in Texas and beyond. However, the tension between extension of the VRA versus *expansion* of the VRA put Jordan at odds with several of her Texas Democratic colleagues, as well as her colleagues in the CBC. Several CBC members were against efforts to expand the VRA and did not want to jeopardize the possibility of the VRA

---

[28] Texas was so fearful of having to succumb to the oversight of the Justice Department for voting and election laws that legislators hastily passed their own statewide bilingual ballot bill in an effort to forestall their inclusion in the federal bill.

[29] The Fifteenth Amendment protection "is not limited to black people. Any denial of voting rights, on the ground of race or color, would contravene the Fifteenth Amendment" (Rogers, 1998: 243). Jordan recognized that "race or color" was not precise and therefore could include Spanish-language voters.

[30] Under the law Jordan proposed, the recognition of low voter turnout and large concentrations of non-English speakers was part of the updated expansion of the law. If voter turnout in any given area was less than 50 percent, a 5 percent concentration of non-English-speaking voters would trigger the preclearance sections of the Voting Rights Act, and the use of bilingual ballots would be necessary (Rogers, 1998).

extension.[31] Jordan, from the state of Texas, which had a sizable and growing Latinx electorate, understood the importance and necessity of expanding voting rights efforts. Jordan's CBC colleagues were aware of her ability to negotiate with and persuade her white male Democratic colleagues, as well as use the assistance of Lyndon Johnson when necessary in order to achieve particular policy goals. Therefore, debates with Jordan often felt as if a shadow of power stood behind her while she faced off against her CBC colleagues or other Democratic colleagues.

Jordan's political maneuvering with the expansion of the VRA – cultivating friendships with a diverse group of Democratic legislators, negotiating relationships with northern and urban CBC members, and utilizing her long-standing relationship with LBJ to assist in persuasion efforts – showed her colleagues that she possessed an ability to research, compromise when necessary, persuade her colleagues with her oratorical skills and "eloquence," and separate herself from her colleagues in Texas or even the CBC when necessary.[32] Jordan made friends with powerful legislators in the House as well as the Senate in efforts to move the expanded VRA bill forward. Her relationship with Democratic senator Robert Byrd of West Virginia during this process strengthened considerably and was an example of Jordan's ability to work with legislators who could assist her with the larger goal of legislation for the people.[33] Senator Byrd fought off filibuster attempts to invoke a cloture vote and limit debate on the bill. Byrd reached a compromise bill with his Senate colleagues in order for the legislation to pass. The bill was moved to President Gerald R. Ford's desk for signing on August 6, 1975, just one day before the VRA was set to expire. During her tenure in Congress, Jordan often leaned on the lessens she learned while serving in the Texas statehouse. Her experience finding compromises and building intra- and interparty relationships assisted Jordan once she was in the halls of Congress with the aim of

---

[31] For example, Andrew Young of Georgia, Jordan's only other CBC colleague from the South, favored the inclusion of Mexican Americans in the 1975 bill. However, he wanted to keep general electoral and registration reform out of extension efforts (Rogers, 1998). Young's stance represented the majority of the CBC opinion.

[32] Although Jordan occasionally disagreed with her CBC colleagues on important legislation, during this time she was the most sought-after African American speaker in the nation. Caucus members often invited her to their respective home districts because of her oratorical skills and her ability to mobilize and inspire voters and draw crowds into the political sphere (Rogers, 1998).

[33] Jordan thread a particularly fine needle of political maneuvering with her white Southern colleagues. Her successes were explained away as political protection by her mentor LBJ, when, in fact, much of her ability to achieve policy gains was due to her political savvy and ability to build multifaceted coalitions with several different types of legislators across regional and policy interests.

enacting political change. The skills and relationships Jordan attained at the state level translated into political wins and national policy.

Part of the legacy of Barbara Jordan was her ability to work with her colleagues on varying interests and priorities, from her days in the Texas statehouse to working the halls of Congress in Washington, DC. Much like Stacey Abrams decades later in the Georgia statehouse, Jordan often found a point of shared commonality to push legislation forward. Whether working with a northern CBC colleague or a conservative southern Democrat, Jordan was able to use her knowledge of the law, political processes, negotiation tactics to assist in her legislative victories, and the larger goal of working toward the good. Her understanding of the needs of those looking to the government to provide equitable resources – whether Texans, Black people, the working poor, or women – gave Jordan an in-depth appreciation of the power of local, state, and federal government programs. Her tenure in the Texas statehouse created a foundation for much of the policy Jordan would champion throughout her time in Congress.

Keynote Address at Democratic National Convention, 1976: A Voice for Justice

"Every Democratic Party chip is on you." Bob Strauss spoke these words to Jordan before her 1976 DNC speech.[34] Jordan's oratorical skills and intellectual clarity were well known and well respected by her colleagues, even if begrudgingly. Jordan had already displayed her unwavering commitment to the future and promise of American democracy during the Nixon impeachment process. Her ability to connect with her congressional colleagues, as well as with Americans more broadly, made her an ideal Democratic leader to deliver such an important address that year. Several governors were upset about her selection because obviously they wanted the coveted keynote spot. Many know the beginning of Jordan's now famous speech, which ranks among the top ten best political speeches in American history (Sherman, 2007). Jordan's confidants initially worried that the beginning of her speech would ostracize some or appear presumptuous. They were wrong. Jordan began her now infamous speech, which brought Democrats to their feet on several occasions, with, "It was 144 years ago that members of the Democratic Party first met in convention to select their presidential candidate. Since that time, Democrats have continued to convene once every four years to draft a party platform and nominate a presidential candidate. Our meeting this week is a continuation of

---

[34] "A Voice for Justice Dies" was the headline of the *Houston Chronicle* the day after Jordan died (Sherman, 2007: 89).

that tradition. But there is something special about tonight. What is different? What is special? I, Barbara Jordan, am a keynote speaker."

The thirty-minute, largely nonpartisan keynote created the "emotional rationale for the unity the party so desperately needed and wanted by penetrating the special-interest arguments and baroque barriers that had been built up over time" (Rogers, 1998: 7). Jordan was the first African American woman to make a keynote address to a national convention of a major political party. In the opening moments of her speech she declared, "My presence here is one additional bit of evidence that the American Dream need not forever be deferred." Jordan's speech quickly became an integral part of the American political cannon of historic speeches. Her calls for electoral expansion, not just protection, set the stage for larger conversations pertaining to increased civil liberties for all, including growing immigrant populations. Her understanding of national policy as it relates to the diverse nuances and needs of all fifty states was a larger contextualization of her understanding of the interplay between state-level and national-level politics and policy. Jordan's focus on providing legislation for the masses, not just her constituents, all while working with executive-level leadership, assisted in her legislative successes. In addition, her keen observations of her colleagues as well as her sharpened political instincts over the years enabled her to use the moment of her DNC speech to reiterate the Democratic Party's commitment to its common destiny and the role of its members as public servants. Jordan stated, "A nation is formed by the willingness of each of us to share in the responsibility for upholding the common good." Her words turned into marching orders for the Democratic Party to resolve internal strife and coalesce around a presidential candidate so that the party could get back to the business of representing and working on behalf of the American people.

Roughly fifteen years later, when Jordan delivered another keynote speech at the 1992 DNC, her speech had a considerably different tone. "Friends of the Democratic Party, the American Dream is not dead. It is not dead! It is gasping for breath, but it is not dead. We can applaud that statement and know that there is no time to waste because the American Dream is slipping away from far too many people" (Sherman, 2007: 41). Jordan had given herself time to reflect on her successes, and defeats, as well as the limitations of the American experiment. Time had sobered Jordan to a certain extent, but her belief in the American Dream was still evident. Jordan's pragmatic patriotism extended late into her life. She never gave up on her desire for a transformation of the American Dream. She exemplified what it meant to be a true patriot, one who believes in and supports her country all while understanding the fault lines and limitations. Most importantly, Jordan believed in the nation's ability to change, expand, and become more inclusive. She believed in the government's ability to do more for families and help them rise from their personal circumstance, just as government programs had done for her family. Jordan fundamentally believed in the role of formal electoral politics in helping Black Americans vote for and elect leaders to represent them both descriptively and substantively.

Compared with modern-day politicians, Barbara Jordan did not stay in public office long: only three two-year terms on the state level and three two-year terms on the federal level. Her entire tenure in electoral politics on the state and federal levels was twelve years. During that time, she witnessed the power of coalition building, legislative victories, and the changing of public opinion. Jordan worked with other southerners to find common ground on legislation, with CBC members to advance democracy for Black Americans, and most importantly with other Black women in Congress to help increase the Black electorate and provide substantive policies for Black and other marginalized families across the nation.

After Jordan voluntarily left public office in 1979, when she retired from electoral office, until her death in 1996, she served as a distinguished professor at the Lyndon B Johnson School of Public Affairs at the University of Texas at Austin, holding the Lyndon B. Johnson Centennial Chair in National Policy. Jordan's eloquence and the way she was able to do her job as a representative despite the racial and gender barriers garnered not only the attention of Black Americans but their admiration as well. Black people in the United States are keenly aware of the challenges of a prominent, successful, "articulate, and intellectually ambitious woman like Barbara Jordan, even if they have never set foot on the marble floors of the Capitol or even touched their feet on the soil in Washington, DC."[35] Jordan was a towering figure in Texas politics, in Washington, and throughout Black America. The legacy of Jordan's eloquence and intellect extended far beyond her fifteen minutes and the 1976 DNC. Her political efforts laid a foundation for Black women in electoral politics at the state and federal levels. Her interactions with US presidents also created an early blueprint for the likes of Kamala Harris and Stacey Abrams some fifty years later. Both Harris and Abrams, sharp legal minds who at various points in their careers have channeled the oratorical eloquence and precision of Jordan, have held higher electeds to account and dedicated their professional careers to

---

[35] Paula Giddings (1975) further states, "To black people in general, Barbara Jordan is the serious politician who gets things done with a minimum of empty rhetoric and ostentatious posturing. She plays the game the way it is played, without apologizing for it, without amoral excesses, and with a great deal of success. She is the kind of woman we all have known in our lives – her eye on the sparrow, taking care of business. And her manner of speaking probably holds more significance to Black people than Whites" (Rogers, 1998: 273).

the advancement of American democratic ideals. Harris, as the highest-ranking Black woman in the history of the nation, solidly rests on the shoulders of Barbara Jordan. Abrams, as a daughter of the US South who came closest to achieving an executive electoral victory in the South, also stands on the shoulders of Jordan and her democracy-building efforts.

Barbara Jordan's tenure in the House of Representatives was relatively short-lived because those were the terms that she selected. A master of her own fate, the eternal captain of her own ship.

4 Stacey Abrams: Wisdom, Justice, and Moderation

Political scientists and scholars of Black politics have attempted to dissect the nuances of Black political leadership for almost a century, and much of the scholarship has focused on Black male politicians on local, state, and federal levels.[36] There have been myriad Black male mayors and members of Congress, almost a dozen US senators, and three Black men elected governor of US states. To date, no Black woman has ever served as governor in the United States, and only two Black women have been elected to the US Senate. However, the lack of top-level positions held by Black women is not an indication of their contributions to the democratic processes in the United States. More recently, robust scholarship focusing on Black women (as candidates, elected officials, and voters) has expanded our understanding of Black women as political actors and leaders (Brown, 2014; Dowe, 2020; Smooth, 2014). Stacey Abrams has emerged as a Black political leader who represents people and policy, not just in Georgia or the US South but also across the United States, as Black Americans continue to fight for the franchise and equal representation in the American polity.[37]

This section lays out the contributions of arguably one of the most important political figures when it comes to twenty-first-century conversations about electoral expansion, protection, and American democracy more broadly. Like Hamer and Jordan before her, Abrams built a foundation working for and alongside Black people in her state. Both in and outside of politics, Abrams worked to expand voting rights, establish grassroots foundations, build myriad coalitions, and negotiate and compromise across party lines. She serves as an eloquent voice articulating the necessity and urgency of America's democratic project. Her efforts are a continuation of generations of work that preceded her,

---

[36] Wisdom, Justice, Moderation is the motto of the state of Georgia.

[37] It should be noted that Stacey Abrams's work has been recognized internationally, as she, just like fellow Georgian Dr. Martin Luther King, Jr., before her, was nominated for a Nobel Peace Prize – she in 2021 for her organizing and registration efforts in Georgia and several other US states during the 2020 US presidential election.

and it is her understanding of that legacy that has aided her in working toward the intended ideals of the United States.

Most Americans were introduced to Stacey Abrams in 2018 when she won the Democratic nomination for governor of Georgia, beating Stacey Evans with more than 76 percent of the vote.[38] Abrams faced several obstacles during the primary and general phases of the election cycle, including convincing Georgia voters, both Black and white, that a talented and prepared Black female candidate could actually win statewide in the US South, a feat not previously accomplished. Abrams also had to overcome institutional barriers put in place by Republican leadership, which sought to limit Black access to the ballot. Her Republican opponent in the general election, Brian Kemp, was the sitting secretary of state, a position from which he did not resign while running for governor. In his role as secretary of state, he was also directly in charge of the policies and mechanisms that governed electoral access for counties throughout the state. In the 2018 election, Kemp held two simultaneous roles: that of candidate and also facilitator of the electoral process.

The Beginning

Abrams moved from Mississippi to Georgia at the age of fifteen with her mother, a librarian, and her father, a shipyard worker. Abrams graduated from Spelman College in 1995 and then received her MA at the LBJ School of Public Affairs at UT Austin. While attending the LBJ School, Abrams enrolled in law school at Yale University. During this time, *Hopwood* v. *Texas* was litigated, which would decrease the number of students of color at the University of Texas. Using her skills as an innovator, Abrams created her own program between the LBJ School and Yale with the assistance of Max Sherman, a dean at the LBJ School and a friend of the late Barbara Jordan.[39]

Abrams started thinking about public office during her Spelman years. The first time she ran for office was for freshman class secretary. During this time, Abrams was involved in Rodney King protests the summer between her freshman and sophomore years. She was appointed sophomore year to the Student Government Association (SGA) as the social media specialist. During her sophomore year, she interned with Atlanta mayor Maynard Jackson's office as a coordinator with the Office of Youth Services.[40] At the time, Abrams was thinking about the role of mayor as a path to public service. She was interested

---

[38] Source: nyti.ms/49Ayb8p.

[39] For a more detailed account of the political origins of Abrams, see Abrams (2019). *Lead from the Outside*. New York: Picador.

[40] Abrams led protests and organized students in response to the racial unrest in the city and the nation. Abrams accused Mayor Jackson of not doing enough for young people in the city of

in the mayor's office in part because (1) the job involved organizing young people to talk about gang violence and poverty issues, and (2) it was the biggest job Abrams had ever heard of for a Black person.[41] Being able to respond to immediate needs seemed like the pinnacle of opportunity for Abrams at the time. Douglas Wilder had already been elected governor in Virginia, but there had been no Black women in executive-level political jobs, especially in the US South. During her sophomore year, Abrams ran for vice president of the SGA and won. She served as SGA vice president during her junior year and as SGA president her senior year.

Abrams was less involved in the types of Hamer-level grassroots organizing at this time and was more interested in a Jordan-level understanding of who could solve the problem the fastest and who could leverage power. This approach to political organizing came in the form of Abrams's work with a community bank. However, like Hamer, Abrams was concerned with economic issues as a means of better understanding the political plight of Black Americans. In addition, Abrams's interest in how power is attained and leveraged arose when she was attending the LBJ School and questions surrounding the diversity (or lack thereof) of the faculty became an issue. Having seen how protest politics was one means of enacting change, Abrams decided to position herself on the hiring committee at the university in order to make change from within. From Abrams's college years and into the beginning of her career, she possessed a combination of Hamer's and Jordan's understandings of insider and outsider politics and how to effect change.

The Political Rise of Abrams

Abrams first ran for state representative when there was an open seat in 2006. In that election she faced two male opponents, and one of her opponents had represented a part of the district before it had been gerrymandered. In Georgia, in order to be victorious in an election, one must win 50 percent plus 1; Abrams received 50.1 percent of the vote and avoided a runoff. This election was notable because Abrams was not, by many Atlantans' estimation, "from the community,"

Atlanta, and although Abrams lost the argument with the mayor and his administration, when Jackson created the Office of Youth Services, he hired Abrams for the job.

[41] The observation by Abrams makes the argument pertaining to *descriptive representation* necessary and relevant. It is important for people to see themselves represented demographically in various levels of political office. If you can see it, you can be it. Therefore, the election of Kamala Harris as the first Black vice president of the United States means something descriptively for the future of women in political office, African Americans, Asian Americans, and all of the varying demographics encompassed in Harris. The more complex debates extend to substantive representation, that is, whether or not your elected officials represent your political preferences and interests. For a more detailed discussion, see Brown-Dean, 2019.

in that she had lived and worked outside the state at various points in her life. Because of this reality, she ran as a technocrat and highlighted her work at varying levels of city, state, county, and federal government. Abrams campaigned diligently and created the "Ask me a question" segment during her campaign whereby voters were able to ask her about how government works. Abrams was elected in 2006, served in the Georgia statehouse, and built a reputation for helping other legislators in various ways through legislation research, writing, and bipartisan negotiating. Abrams was also good at fundraising, bill reading, and answering questions from her colleagues and constituents. Because of this, she was then elected deputy whip by her peers after her first year and gained even more responsibility.

In 2010, Abrams ran and was elected to serve as minority leader in the Georgia statehouse, where she served for the next seven years. Abrams's first year was a redistricting year, and under Abrams's leadership, for the first time in a very long time, House Democrats all voted together against a gerrymandered map. Abrams's ability to explain the larger collective goal to a diverse group of Democratic legislators was something Hamer often did with her organizing colleagues across the state of Mississippi. It is also something Jordan was able to articulate to her CBC and Democratic colleagues in Congress.

In 2012, Abrams was able to increase the number of Democratic seats in the Georgia statehouse, thus preventing the Georgia Republican Party from attaining a supermajority. In 2014, Democrats did not lose a single seat. In 2016, Democrats even picked up seats. And in 2018, Democrats picked up fourteen seats in the House and Senate. During Abrams's tenure as House minority leader, most of her time was spent going after less viable seats and achieving larger goals for Democratic Party control, which would inevitably help all marginalized people in the state. During Abrams's entire tenure in the statehouse, the Republican Party controlled the governorship. Abrams realized that the intersection between city needs and state-level leadership was limited if the final and deciding factor rested with the governor of Georgia. It was then that Abrams decided to run statewide for the highest office in the state, in hopes of becoming the first Black female elected governor in the history of the state and in the history of the United States.

What Is Unique about Georgia Politics?

The city of Atlanta was looked at as a focal point of politics because of the large minority population as well as its economic-engine status in the Deep South. The number of Fortune 500 companies in Atlanta, the transportation matrix, and former mayor Maynard Jackson's investments created the deepest concentration of Black millionaires in the country. Georgia is an important US southern state because Atlanta is an economic and political center in the South. Thus, organizing in Georgia facilitates the ability to knit together coalitions across the region.

Abrams has argued that being Black in Atlanta is not the same as being Black in Macon or rural Georgia. One-third of rural Georgia consists of marginalized groups, and in order to think through economic and social justice issues, one must take into account suburban, exurban, and rural areas and have leadership that understands those intersections. Georgia forces one to consider the multi-strand identities of all residents and understand how they intersect. Georgia comprises eleven million people, and unlike Alabama and Mississippi, Georgia (like Texas) is a diverse state in the US South, made up of not just Black and white but also significant Latinx and Asian American populations. Successful politicians cannot just focus on Black and white groups and policy needs; their success demands the incorporation of other communities. Abrams was the first leader to hire multiple staff leaders full-time and year-round who represented Georgia's racial and ethnic diversity. Abrams hired from all communities of color, and the various racial and ethnic communities had *paid* representation in Abrams's office when she became state representative. Abrams understood the necessity of merging the economic and the political. Her office needed full-time employees to respond to the needs of Georgians beyond the end of the session. Politics and policy were a year-round effort, as was racial and ethnic representation.

Building a Campaign

Data show that when Black women run, they can actually win. For Black women, running on the statehouse level presents a necessary pipeline to running for higher office, most notably Congress (Brown, 2014). Just as Shirley Chisholm and Barbara Jordan began their careers in their respective statehouses before heading to the House of Representatives, Stacey Abrams also began her career in the Georgia statehouse before running for governor of Georgia. When Black women run, they often need different coalitions to win. Even if running in a primarily Black district, Black female candidates must often build multiracial coalitions as well as introduce new voters into the political sphere (Dowe, 2020).[42] Black women running for office also often need more money and

---

[42] According to Dowe (2020), for Stacey Abrams, three factors determined her decision: (1) radical imagination, (2) ambition, and (3) marginalization. For a more detailed summary, see Dowe (2020), "Resisting Marginalization: Black Women's Political Ambition and Agency." *PS: Political Science & Politics*, 53(4): 697–702.

people to invest in them. Because there has never been a Black woman elected governor of a state in the history of the nation,[43] and only two Black women who have ever been elected to the US Senate – Carol Moseley Braun (D-IL) in 1992 and Kamala Harris (D-CA) in 2016 – the model of Black women electeds on the statewide level is limited. Abrams's incredibly close electoral success can and should serve as a model and blueprint for Black women seeking statewide office.

Abrams presented bold, inclusive policies that were more progressive than those of her predecessors, but not so leftist as to alienate moderate Democratic voters, both Black and white.[44] Abrams also recognized the changing demographics in Georgia, with Latinx and Asian Americans settling in the state (Noe-Bustamante and Budiman, 2020),[45] as well as Black reverse migration – that is, Black families and retirees returning to the US South after a generation or more. Abrams realized that Georgia politics no longer reflected a dichotomous relationship between Black and white voters, as had been the historical reality. Her ability to recognize the increased racial and ethnic diversity within the state and, more specifically, within the electorate led to her active inclusion of Latinx and Asian American voters and broke new political ground for the Democratic Party throughout the state.[46] Similarly to Jordan, Abrams's understanding of the necessity of interracial (and sometimes interparty) coalition building facilitated her successes in organizing and legislating within the southern Democratic political structure.

When Black women are in elected office, they tend to stick to an agenda and execute their goals in specific and deliberate ways (Brown, 2014).

---

[43] On the presidential map of the United States, states are often broken into red states (Republican Party) and blue states (Democratic Party). However, I argue that all states are red states with blue cities. Every four years when electing a president, we see whether those blue cities can turn an entire state blue. At the county level, a "liberal" state is mostly red with a few deep pockets of blue. Therefore, when candidates of color, Black women especially, run for statewide office, their challenges are quite steep. They must raise money to run statewide, convince voters to overcome their racial and gender biases, and present their executive-level qualifications. Without a large number of women who have previously held statewide office, elected or appointed, Black female candidates face additional burdens when seeking higher office.

[44] There is an assumption that most Black voters are progressive. However, since roughly 90 percent of Black voters are registered with the Democratic Party, the ideological diversity of Black voters is widespread. Black voters are not inherently progressive, especially in the US South. Much of the widespread policy diversity among Black voters is "trapped" within the Democratic Party, largely because the Republican Party has chosen to cast its lot with a more white nationalist ideology (Frymer, 1999). Black voters must also keep the realities of white political needs and wants in the forefront of their minds while voting. As strategic voters, Black in the electorate think widely about their ideals as well as those of whites in the electorate.

[45] Source: pewrsr.ch/3vUe0o6.

[46] Abrams's multiethnic voter registration efforts across the state directly resulted in the electoral success of two Democratic US senators in the January 2021 runoff elections.

They also tend to work on broader committees and represent a wide range of their constituents (Carroll and Sanbonmatsu, 2013). When Abrams was in the Georgia statehouse, she represented the Eighty-Ninth District, which was roughly 60 percent Black, based primarily in Atlanta, and in the 95th percentile of household income compared with the rest of the state, with almost 50 percent of the district possessing at least a bachelor's degree. Abrams did not represent a rural or relatively poor district, but as a Black female candidate and representative, she needed to engage constituents in policy discussions that extended beyond their immediate circumstances.[47]

For Black female candidates to succeed, they must often articulate an array of policy issues and reach a broad swath of voters, in both political discussions and fundraising (Dowe, 2020). For many Black female candidates, fundraising challenges are persistent, especially when they're running for statewide office. Many Black Americans do not have a long history of donating to political campaigns (Brown, 2014). Black Americans *do* donate to charitable organizations at higher rates than other racial and ethnic groups.[48] However, *political* giving has not become a calcified widespread behavior within the community. Black Americans have a long history of donating to their religious institutions, family members, and organizations within their communities, but the financial contributions to politics have not been as robust and consistent. Abrams was able to circumvent some of the obstacles that often limit Black women's ability to wage a successful primary bid through her skilled fundraising abilities, clear articulation of a diverse set of policy proposals, and an inclusive message and organizing apparatus.[49]

Most Black female electeds remain at the local level due to the financial constraints as well as the overall belief that Black women cannot lead in the same ways as their white female, Black male, or white male colleagues (Smooth, 2014). An assessment of Black women who have been elected to Congress or various offices throughout their states shows that many of them began their careers in their respective statehouses (Brown, 2014). Thus, the importance of the statehouse as a launching pad for Black women in electoral politics cannot be overstated (Carroll and Sanbonmatsu, 2013). That Abrams followed the statehouse path of her predecessors Shirley Chisholm and Barbara Jordan should be noted. That Abrams decided not to run for the US

---

[47] Source: bit.ly/3vZq7jF.

[48] Source: www.washingtonpost.com/business/2020/12/11/black people-prioritize-philanthropy/.

[49] When Abrams ran in her Democratic primary against former state representative Stacey Evans, a white woman, Abrams won 153 out of 159 counties across the state during the primary. Abrams received 424,305 votes to Evans's 130,784 votes.

House of Representatives but to aim for the governor's mansion instead illustrates a few things. First, Abrams assembled a different set of coalitions in comparison with her predecessors. Running for Congress requires a different set of multiracial coalition efforts. Second, the fundraising infrastructure needed to run for statewide office is significantly larger than that needed for congressional fundraising. Lastly, the cross-cutting policy proposals necessary for a statewide run must reflect the widespread political diversity that exists within the Democratic Party as well as independents across the state.

As Dowe (2020) argues, a political imagination is necessary for Black female electeds and candidates. Abrams saw the possibility of increasing the electorate by actively including Latinx and Asian American voters in policy discussions. Abrams also clearly understood the "varying shades of blue" present in Georgia and presented a diverse portfolio of pragmatic policy proposals, ranging from tax reform to criminal justice to transportation, for Democratic voters. The Black–white binary is a calcified concept in American democracy and American politics because centuries of white supremacy and anti-Blackness have pervaded most policy discussions and prescriptions. However, in order to understand a more nuanced picture of American politics, it is necessary to include other growing racial and ethnic groups whose multidimensional partisan ties prompt complex discussions about possibilities for coalition building, increased voter participation, and policy prescriptions.

The 2018 Campaign

When Stacey Abrams decided to run for the governorship of Georgia, she knew it would be an uphill effort. There was no blueprint for a Black woman running and succeeding in that endeavor. She did have the policy foundation as a legislator, having served in the Georgia statehouse for over a decade. However, executive-level leadership differs from leadership over one's colleagues, as Abrams had experienced as minority leader in the statehouse. Similarly to Barbara Jordan, Abrams was a trailblazer as a Black female candidate in the US South. And like Fannie Lou Hamer, Abrams utilized her ability to work with Black female-led organizations across the state to share a vision for multiracial economic and political advancement of marginalized groups in the state. And as with both of her predecessors, her electoral success hinged on increased inclusion of Black Democratic voters. To bring her message to the masses, Abrams created a far-reaching campaign that involved educating voters about the issues, a robust fundraising apparatus across the country,[50] and an articulation of the micro and macro stakes of electoral registration and participation.

Abrams knew that if she were to be successful in a statewide race, the franchise would need to be extended equitably to all Georgia residents. According to Chisholm, "Of course, all this theoretical discussion should not lead anyone to lose sight of the three basic elements of political action – registration, financing, and campaigning" (Chisholm, [1970] 2009: 164). In order for Abrams to fight against the reign of the Republican Party – with its organizational efforts, its ability to raise money within and outside the state and campaign on fearmongering and status quo politics, and its historical and institutional disenfranchisement efforts – Abrams knew she would need to not only incorporate new voters into the electoral sphere but also decrease barriers for those who wished to participate in electoral politics, all while dealing with biases inherent in being a female candidate for executive office (Carroll and Sanbonmatsu, 2013).

There are stereotypes and biases that female candidates encounter when running for higher office, as well as different sets of stereotypes and biases that Black candidates face when seeking higher and/or executive office (Carroll and Sanbonmatsu, 2013; Greer, 2016a). Abrams knew what Carroll and Sanbonmatsu (2013) argue, that "gender inequality in politics primarily stems from gender inequities that[51] can be found in society". Therefore, in order for Abrams to succeed at the statewide level, she would need to attempt to decrease the inequities that made it more difficult for Black women, and several other marginalized groups, in the state of Georgia to participate in electoral political processes.

Abrams's priority was making sure all Georgians had access to the ballot. One sign of a healthy democracy is free and fair elections, something Fannie Lou Hamer, Ella Baker, and so many other Black leaders of civil rights groups had fought tirelessly to secure for Black people, other marginalized groups in Mississippi, and Americans across the South more broadly. Abrams wanted to make sure that Georgians had equal access to opportunities to engage in electoral politics without additional barriers such as long lines and obstacles

---

[50] Abrams's ability to fundraise, as a Black woman, created a new model for candidates throughout the country. Abrams was able to lay out her policy agenda, previous credentials, and ambitions for herself and marginalized groups in a way that inspired voters across Georgia (and the United States more broadly) to donate to her campaign. Abrams was unapologetic about her ability to fundraise. Indeed, Abrams's tenure as a lawyer assisted in creating a foundation of well-off voters who wished to invest in her campaign (Dowe, 2020). However, Abrams also had a message that resonated with middle- and working-class voters, which in turn inspired them to donate to her campaign, no matter how humble the contribution.

[51] Carroll and Sanbonmatsu, 2013: 8.

to absentee voting and language accessibility for non-English speakers. However, the Republican Party in Georgia (similarly to the national Republican Party) knew that increased or equal access to the ballot does not favor their candidates. Therefore, the Georgia Republican Party made entrée into the political process even more difficult during the 2018 election. Fearmongering, misinformation, and expunging lifelong voters from the scrolls were just some of the techniques used to decrease Democratic political power as well as Abrams's chances of becoming governor of Georgia.

Ultimately, the efforts of Brian Kemp and the Republican Party worked. Abrams lost the election to Kemp 50.2 percent to 48.8 percent, the difference of roughly 50,000 votes.[52] Republicans have controlled the Georgia governorship since 2002, even with robust voter turnout in Democratic stronghold cities like Atlanta, Macon, Augusta, Savannah, and Columbus. Because of the Republican- (read: Kemp-) controlled electoral process and the latent institutional barriers that persist for women, Black people, and Black female candidates, Abrams fell just short of becoming the nation's first-ever elected Black female governor (Waxman, 2020).[53]

Despite these blatant attempts to undermine democracy, Abrams was able to use her years of organizing experience to wage the most credible statewide run for governor by a Black woman that the United States has ever seen. Never before had a Black female candidate raised money and inspired voters across race, class, and locale within a state. Abrams connected with voters in cities, suburbs, and rural areas; she articulated a diverse set of policies that resonated with upper-, middle-, and working-class voters; and she incorporated Latinx and Asian American voters in her detailed analysis of racial equity, political participation, and democratic inclusion. Abrams established a fundraising base, articulated her leadership qualifications as minority leader in the Georgia statehouse, and presented a new vision for Georgia that I define as "pragmatic progressivism" – that is, understanding the ideological realities of Georgia as a southern state. Abrams was well aware of the incremental inclinations of voters. Her policy proposals suggested a path toward greater democratic inclusion without falling prey to unrealistic policy proposals that had no chance of being adopted. Her pragmatic vision for Georgia was rooted in her understanding of American political development and democratic promise. Like Hamer and Jordan, who preceded her in southern electoral politics and organizing, Abrams worked with other Black women and Black-led organizations in order to accomplish her policy, voter registration, and expansive democratic goals.

---

[52] Source: nyti.ms/3TUqrbe.
[53] For a more detailed account of the 2018 gubernatorial race, see Abrams (2020), *Our Time Is Now.*

What made Abrams's candidacy so compelling to Georgia voters was her widespread appeal to progressive, moderate, and conservative Democrats, as well as first-time voters. During her tenure in the Georgia statehouse, Abrams served on committees ranging from Appropriations, Ethics, Judiciary (noncivil), Rules, and Ways and Means. She also helped pass legislation pertaining to tax exemptions, amendments to the HOPE Scholarship, and increasing the age for child restraints.

In November 2018, Abrams narrowly lost to Brian Kemp and the Republican Party in a race that most political experts analyzed as deeply corrupt and a systemic effort to extinguish the rights of Black and other Democratic voters in counties across the state. The instances of voter suppression are well documented. For example, voters who had voted in the same polling location arrived on Election Day to find their names missing from the voting scrolls; provisional ballots unavailable at polling locales; polling stations with machines missing power cords; polling stations without sufficient numbers of ballots; new machines not being delivered to primarily Black and Democratic districts; and long lines to vote exceeding six or more hours.[54] The issue of voter suppression has been and continues to be a barrier for Black American political participation. Just as Hamer and Jordan attempted to circumvent the ways that Black Americans were excluded from the electoral process, Abrams faced voter suppression in the modern era. At times, politicians and political parties have been successful in subverting the democratic process by introducing new barriers to voting, whether misinformation and disinformation or literal barriers such as police enforcement, vigilante intimidation, or failure to provide adequate materials and machinery necessary for electoral participation.

Abrams's approach to organizing is an extension of Fannie Lou Hamer's efforts and asks the question, "How do you provide direct service to communities?" In Abrams's estimation, there is a difference between groups that organize *in* community and Abrams's approach, which is organizing *for* community. Years later, when Abrams began Fair Fight, the goal of the organization was to organize people as well as tackle voter suppression and points of power. Fair Count, another organization that Abrams founded, got people to complete the census and also gain awareness of the decennial census. Abrams's goal, similar to Hamer's and Jordan's, was to get close to the points of power and pain and use her leverage to open doors in order to assist Black people and marginalized communities. And similar to the two women before her, Abrams's goal was also to increase Black voter registration and participation.[55]

---

[54] Sources: bit.ly/3JkSYSL; bit.ly/3UmFICf; bit.ly/3JncHAZ.

[55] Some of the organizations that Abrams began dealt with issues that would help marginalized communities throughout the state. Abrams created Nourish, which supplied fresh water to

Abrams's loss was a loss for so many across the country who had contributed time and money in hopes of electing the first Black female governor in US history (Hooker, 2017). However, unlike many of her male counterparts who experienced electoral losses in 2018 and went into the private sector or accepted jobs at varying political levels, Abrams remained in Georgia and continued her work. Those who did not pay close attention to the Georgia gubernatorial race in 2018 soon became familiar with Abrams after the election when she founded Fair Fight to promote fair elections around the country. Through her efforts with that organization, Abrams worked to ensure that Georgia and several other key battleground states across the country increased the inclusivity of their electoral practices and registered citizens to ensure their ability to participate in the 2020 presidential elections. This grassroots work contributed to a Democratic presidential nominee winning Georgia in 2020, the first time since 1992. Her efforts also ensured the wins of two Democratic US senators from the state of Georgia in the January 2021 runoff elections, positions that have changed the composition of the US Senate and assisted Democratic President Joe Biden with enacting his agenda (Cohn, 2021).[56]

The rippling effect of Abrams's loss, albeit a loss of the governorship, allowed Abrams to focus her efforts on continued ballot access for Georgians and voters in other swing states across the United States. Citizens in states as diverse as Arizona, Pennsylvania, and Wisconsin benefited from the efforts of Abrams and her organizations that focused on voter access in the 2020 presidential elections. As with Hamer, setbacks stung, but their effects were never long-lasting. The work continued. And similarly to Jordan, Abrams's ability to articulate a vision of American democracy and inclusion allowed her to persuade Americans across the country and appeal to their greater angels in pursuit of political inclusivity and electoral equity.

Abrams also ran for Georgia governor in 2022 and again came up short. In this particular election, she faced the uphill battle of running against Brian Kemp, the incumbent.[57] Although her registration efforts across the state of Georgia were robust, the efforts, practices, and policies of the Republican Party

---

babies. Like Fannie Lou Hamer's farm cooperative, this endeavor ultimately failed due to lack of capital. Abrams also created the Now Account, which served minority- and women-owned businesses by increasing supplier diversity efforts in order to fund these businesses and expand their access to capital. These projects showed Abrams that organizing and money can create sustainable differences.

[56] Without the two Democratic senators from Georgia, Joe Biden would not have unified two branches of the federal government (Democratic control of the presidency along with the House and Senate) and would not have been able to pass any legislation or ensure any confirmations to his cabinet.

[57] The Brian Kemp campaign practiced similar unsavory tactics during the 2018 Republican primary. His antics during the primary as sitting secretary of state left his own party with feelings

aimed at disenfranchising voters were even stronger. What Abrams's two gubernatorial runs exposed was just how much soil still needs to be tilled in our efforts toward electoral equality and inclusion. Just as Fannie Lou Hamer and Barbara Jordan articulated fifty to sixty years prior, the work for marginalized groups remains, and we must continue to fight, organize, and speak out on behalf of Americans who cannot ... even in the midst of institutional and structural barriers.

Moving Forward

Part of Abrams's appeal to voters across the state of Georgia was her refusal to present herself as anything other than an intellectual Black woman who understood the nuances of policy and could translate that understanding to her fellow Georgians. Shirley Chisholm stated that "for our freedom struggle to advance in the political arena, black politicians have to accept their blackness" (Chisholm, [1970] 2009: 162). Part of Abrams's appeal to Black voters was her unapologetic Blackness, from her natural hair and style of dress to her ability to build coalitions and her fiercely independent nature.[58] Abrams articulated a political and economic vision for all Georgians that was attainable and realistic for Black Georgians. She battled with Republican legislators to make sure funding reached Black communities; read bills thoroughly to find hidden proposals that would take away rights and resources from Black communities; and, when necessary, compromised with those across the aisle to maximize the benefits for those she served. Abrams's efforts to register and incorporate all Georgians into the electoral sphere are reminiscent of Hamer's efforts some sixty years earlier in Mississippi. Both women recognized the deliberate ways that their respective states sought to disenfranchise Black voters in overt and covert ways. Abrams also worked alongside other Georgians doing the work of organizing, registering, and educating voters in the state – Black women like Nsé Ufot, CEO of the New Georgia Project; Helen Butler, executive director of the Georgia Coalition for the Peoples' Agenda; and LaTosha Brown, cofounder of the Black Voters Matter Fund, to name just a few.

Abrams's unyielding mission to provide an equal ground for Black citizens in the state of Georgia was also an extension of Barbara Jordan's efforts in Texas and Fannie Lou Hamer's in Mississippi. Sadly, the US South, more than a half a century after Hamer and Jordan, has continued to create ways to limit Black electoral inclusion and the benefits of the full franchise (hence the need for the

---

of mistrust, hence his 2022 gubernatorial primary challenge by former Georgia US senator David Perdue.

[58] For a more nuanced analysis of Black women running as unapologetically Black, see *Sister Style: The Politics of Appearance for Black Women Political Elites* (Brown and Lemi, 2021).

work of organizations like Fair Fight, the New Georgia Project, the Black Voters Fund, and the Georgia Coalition for the Peoples' Agenda, along with several other Black-led organizations). Abrams's efforts in the statehouse, as well as her candidacy for governor, served as an attempt to (1) continue the legacy of Jordan, Hamer, and countless other Black female organizers; (2) build a coalition of voters and change the political imagination of voters through a diverse representation in leadership; and (3) assist Black citizens in a policy and electoral space as their representative.

5 Conclusion

To live in the United States as a Black person is to live in a country whose inception and ethos is that of Black inequality and deliberate exclusion and subjugation. Black people have worked within and around the entrenched system, and in many ways it is as real and powerful as the air we breathe. The invisibility of racism for some white Americans allows them to ignore (consciously and subconsciously) the historic and present-day effects of a system set up explicitly by and for them. As Black women traverse this terrain in attempts to change the fate of not just Black Americans but also marginalized groups writ large, their work and leadership is often rendered invisible because of race, gender, class, and even geography. This Element attempts to provide context for the road traveled by three Black women who have inextricably changed the course of American political history by their strategy, leadership, bravery, and efforts within the American political system.

Fannie Lou Hamer should be remembered as a fearless grassroots organizer and coalition builder who believed not only in the political power of the vote but also in economic independence and self-reliance. It was Hamer's relentless focus on securing the right to vote for Black people in Mississippi, and the broader US South, that solidified Hamer as a patriot willing to put her body on the line in order for others to benefit from the promises of American democracy. Her keen understanding of the interplay between white supremacy, anti-Blackness, patriarchy, and racialized capitalism that purposefully excluded Black people gave her deep insight into US politics as they played out daily on local, state, and federal levels.

Hamer fought tirelessly to provide Black southerners with some of their most basic rights as US citizens. Her attempts to promote political inclusion for Black and white Mississippians stemmed from her beliefs in collective action and humanity. Similarly, Barbara Jordan believed in America as a national community best exemplified in the motto *E pluribus unum* – "Out of many, one." Jordan used more traditional tools in her work toward equity and political inclusion for Black Americans. Her legislation on state and national levels increased Black political participation and representation and also extended rights and liberties to other marginalized groups. Her understanding of the judicial system, as well as the negotiations and compromise needed for the legislative process, aided in her ability to build coalitions within her party among a diverse set of legislators, both northern and southern, Black and non-Black, and urban and rural.

As we consider the lives and work of Hamer and Jordan – the coalitions they built; their political acumen; the ways they used the interplay between local, state, and national politics to further a vision of American unity, equality, and policy that benefits everyone – the phrase E pluribus Stacey is more apropos. Fannie Lou Hamer and Barbara Jordan did not live their lives as victims, although they both suffered considerable defeats in their political careers. However, as Black women working to create a more equitable nation, neither Jordan nor Hamer experienced full triumphs over all odds. They were still Black women of a certain time period, in the United States, fighting against anti-Black racism and systemic patriarchy. Melissa Harris-Perry argued in *Sister Citizen* that "by studying the lives of Black women, we gain important insight into how citizens yearn for and work toward recognition" (2013: 4). Like Hamer and Jordan, Stacey Abrams experienced political defeats and unjust systems during her tenure as minority leader of the Georgia statehouse and as a candidate for governor of Georgia. However, just like her predecessors, Abrams continued with the work, not for the fanfare but for the larger goal of creating a nation that begins to mirror the lofty ideals in its founding documents . . . in tangible ways that help marginalized groups across the nation.

Being a Black woman in the United States is a peculiar circumstance, to at once be considered a threat by one's mere presence and also rendered simultaneously invisible. Black women are also hailed as the keepers of American democracy while viewed by many as nondeserving of basic democratic norms. The past fifty years have given us examples of Black women in the arts and politics, organizing and leadership, and almost all areas of American life. Yet the ceiling of success for Black women because of race and gender is still far too low. The intersection of race, gender, and class in a nation with a long history of bias – and dare I say hatred toward women and Black people, and Black women in particular – makes the idea of Black female leadership one that is difficult to encapsulate.

This Element attempts to answer these questions for anyone hoping to better understand how Black women, especially and explicitly, fit into the narrative of electoral and organizational politics. All three of these women hailed from the US South, a land soaked in the blood of Black Americans' toil and struggle to free themselves from bondage, become citizens in this land, and incorporate themselves into the political world. They did so by working within and around institutions that were created to perpetuate the initial deliberately unequal circumstances of American democracy. The state violence, as well as the deliberate attempts to disenfranchise Black Americans, that existed during the lifetimes of Hamer and Jordan was excavated and reinforced in a twenty-first-century context during Abrams's political tenure. The efforts of Hamer and Jordan to not only survive but also thrive politically are reminiscent of Abrams's in the post–Barack Obama years in America. A social safety net that supported many other Americans was deliberately rolled back in an effort to return to levels of inequity not seen since the early twentieth century (Michener, 2018).

The work and lives of Fannie Lou Hamer, Barbara Jordan, and Stacey Abrams seemed necessary to explore at this political moment. A broad swath of non-Black Americans still largely feel that Black people are doing better than whites (Pew Research Center, 2016). Therefore, the inclusion of Black women in a space where their struggles for equality and political inclusion are contextualized is of great import if we are to tell an accurate tale of American political development. And although Black women tend to overperform at the ballot box and vote at higher percentages than other racial and ethnic groups, they are still grossly underrepresented in electoral office (Brown, 2014; Carroll and Sanbonmatsu, 2013). This Element comes in the wake of Kamala Harris, the first Black vice president of the United States, and roughly fifty years since Shirley Chisholm ran for the presidency on a major party ticket. However, deeper understandings of Black women in the electoral sphere are still warranted.

Throughout this collective journey for Black political liberation, there were personal costs for Fannie Lou Hamer and Barbara Jordan, including their health. Both women died before their mission was complete. They saw significant gains in American democracy due to their specific and direct efforts. However, the American democratic project is far from complete, and neither Jordan nor Hamer lived long enough to see gains in sustained voter inclusion and electoral politics. Black citizens are still being targeted for exclusion in local and federal elections (Lee, 1999: xi). Both Hamer and Jordan sacrificed their bodies for the movement, and both died at the relatively young age of fifty-nine (in 1977 and 1996, respectively). The personal cost both women paid cannot be measured or ever repaid. Hamer and Jordan were both symbols and workers toward Black electoral inclusion (Lee, 1999: xii). So how do we begin to measure the contributions and sacrifices of these two women in the political sphere? One way we can begin to calculate their efforts is by examining the work of Stacey

Abrams throughout the state of Georgia over the past decade. Her organizational efforts pertaining to voter inclusion, coalition building, and mastery of policy affecting Black people and other marginalized groups are a direct outgrowth of the seeds planted by Fannie Lou Hamer and Barbara Jordan decades prior.

To understand our current political moment, we must understand the interconnectedness of Hamer, Jordan, and Abrams and their electoral and organizational efforts and skills. In some cases, these women were incredibly successful – winning office, registering Black voters, pushing the Democratic Party to see and value Black voters. In other cases, these women were unable to overcome the institutional barriers in place that prevent women, Black people, and Black women most specifically from changing the calcified US political system, predicated on white supremacy, anti-Black racism, patriarchy, and racialized capitalism. Therefore, the presence of Black women in US politics serves as a reflection of both the obstacles Black people face in the political arena and their progress in it.

So where do we go from here? Abrams, in addition to many others both inside the electoral space and in organizing spaces, is currently carrying the mantle of Hamer and Jordan. If one observes the tenure of Donald Trump and the racist backlash he ushered in, cultivated, and encouraged, it may appear as if the four pillars of white supremacy, anti-Blackness, patriarchy, and racialized capitalism are impervious to change. Indeed, the darkness that was unleashed and explained away during Trump's presidency sometimes obscured the work being done and the work that had already been done to ensure that the democratic republic could withstand this type of moment in our nation's history. In many ways, Abrams is heralded as having saved the nation. Her efforts organizing and registering voters in key states across the nation assisted Joe Biden in becoming the forty-sixth president of the United States. Her organizing and fundraising efforts assisted candidates in lower-level races and brought a level of Democratic unified government on the federal level in order to assist Biden in his agenda. Her work in Georgia after the November 2020 election is one of the key elements in her legacy of "saving democracy." Abrams, alongside other organizers in Georgia, worked tirelessly to deliver two Democratic US senators in the runoff elections in January 2021 to aid the Democratic Party in securing a slim Senate majority in the Biden era. Abrams's decision to run again for governor of Georgia in 2022 further reflects her commitment to tilling the soil of democracy for Georgians and millions of others affected by the tyranny of the Republican Party and its assaults on marginalized groups. Her work with Fair Fight affected politics in Georgia as well as in more than a dozen states in the North, Midwest, and Southwest.

It has been documented that Hamer often recited this quote: "You can kill a man, but you can't kill ideas."[59] If this statement is indeed true, as Hamer believed, then ideas will transfer from one generation to the next, which will ultimately lead to the freedom of Black people. However, this philosophy works both ways. White supremacy, anti-Black racism, patriarchy, and racialized capitalism are all ideas that did not die out with subsequent generations. As the keepers of those beliefs died out, their ideas did not. Therefore, just as we can promote and strive toward greater inclusion and equity beyond the individuals who have fought for it for centuries, we must remember that there are still forces in the United States working just as tirelessly to uphold the beliefs of inequality and disenfranchisement.

Success for Black people in the United States has been an amalgamation of protest *and* electoral politics on local, state, and national levels. The two strategies have a symbiotic relationship, and both are necessary for the advancement of Black political agendas. Without protest politics, elected leaders are not motivated to work on behalf of the needs and wants of Black people in America. And once electoral gains are achieved, protest politics are often necessary to sustain and maintain those gains. The mid-1960s were a period in which protest (read: radical) politics intersected with electoral politics. As members of SNCC increasingly leaned into a more Black nationalist politic within Black-led organizations, they rejected a widespread integrationist approach and thought about strategies that would most substantively uplift Black people in the United States. Some Black elected officials also began to advocate for the idea of Black Power overtly or tacitly. Shirley Chisholm believed in Black political mobilization from within the system, "a position she derived from experience and studied observation of both history and the surrounding political landscape" (Guild, 2009: 265). Just like Chisholm, Barbara Jordan was also known for her fierce independence in the face of what she felt was right and best for Black people in America. Both Chisholm and Jordan forged uneasy alliances and coalitions at times and made difficult compromises when necessary in order to advance their causes (Guild, 2009). These women worked within the political realm to enact change for Black people and other marginalized groups in America.

Fannie Lou Hamer spent her political career as an insider and outsider working with SNCC as an established organization, yet her age, education status, and class contributed to a persistent outsider status. Hamer's efforts began in the Mississippi Delta and expanded to her activism, civil rights

---

[59] This quote is also attributed to slain civil rights worker and Mississippi NAACP field secretary Medgar Evers as well as the philosopher Socrates.

organizing, and political leadership on the national stage. After organizing Black women to vote, she worked with various civil rights organizations for the advancement of Black political participation. Hamer solidified her national reputation by cofounding the MFDP, which challenged the local Democratic Party's efforts to block Black participation. Although Hamer's writings are not as abundant as those of some elected officials of her time, by dissecting her public speeches, one can glean a clear understanding of her role in feminist politics (as cofounder of the National Women's Political Caucus), Black politics, politics of the US South, and the realigning Democratic Party of the time.

Hamer was influential in incorporating Black Americans into the Democratic Party amid the Civil Rights Movement (Dawson, 1994). Her relationship with President Johnson was unlike that of her contemporary Barbara Jordan. Whereas Jordan utilized LBJ as a mentor and political incubator while in Congress, Hamer's more antagonistic relationship with Johnson further complicates the perception of LBJ not only as an architect of some of the most influential legislation for Black Americans in the twentieth century – the Civil Rights Act of 1964 and the VRA and Immigration and Nationality Act of 1965 – but also as the gatekeeper to Black political inclusion across the US South (Walton et al., 2016).

Jordan hailed from the Lone Star State and often found herself alone when arguing for the Democratic principles in which she believed. Jordan had to distance herself at times from her Texas colleagues and even her CBC colleagues when she needed to fight for the principles that she believed would advance the dignity and inclusion of Black people and all Americans. As a Black woman from the US South, Jordan opened the proverbial floodgates for Black women to be elected throughout the state of Texas and across the South. Jordan was not necessarily known as a "progressive politician"; therefore, her opinions pertaining to public policy issues ranging from immigration to economics must be further examined through varying lenses. As we continue to think about the integration of Black people as full citizens into this country and Democratic Party politics (Carter, 2019), it is essential to understand the ideological diversity among the Black electorate and Black elected officials. Jordan's intricate dance as someone who was inside the realm of electoral politics but also an outsider who needed to agitate and advocate for others placed her in a difficult dual space among her colleagues as a Black female elected official.

Fast-forward half a century, and Stacey Abrams led the charge with the outstanding theme of securing, protecting, and expanding voting rights for all Americans and continuing the fight to push citizens and legislators to help America live up to her promises and ideals. Applying her understanding of electoral politics and grassroots political organizing was Abrams's strategy as a candidate in 2018. It remained her mission after she was defeated in the governor's race, leading to her contributions to Democratic successes in Georgia in the 2020 presidential election and 2021 Senate races. Like Hamer, Abrams practiced what is described as "bridge leadership," activities providing a link between formal organizations and Black communities (Rhodes, 2003). Abrams's political efforts can be seen as a continuation of the legacy of Hamer and Jordan and so many other Black women. Abrams's background in the public, private, and nonprofit spheres in Georgia is a direct continuation of the internal and external political machinations of Hamer and Jordan some fifty years after their efforts. From establishing the New Georgia Project, registering hundreds of thousands of primarily Black Georgians, and cofounding the NOW Account – a nonprofit financial services firm that assists small businesses – to running for governor of Georgia in 2018 and 2022, Abrams reflects the passing of the torch by these two women of the US South. Abrams understood the need for both insider and outsider political tactics and relationships in order to increase electoral inclusion for Black Georgians and other marginalized groups in the state.

As Jordan stated, "We are a people in a quandary about the present. We are a people in search of our future. We are a people in search of a national community"[60] (Sherman, 2007: 33). It is the "national community" that makes the work of these three women so powerful, not just in the US South but also throughout the nation. Jordan, Hamer, and Abrams were able to articulate an inclusive vision that extended beyond their own personal ambitions. Hamer was often described as having a "voice that moved all who heard her," just like Jordan and Abrams (Bracey, 2011). These Black women worked inside politics to help move the cause of racial and political inclusion forward. Hamer was quoted as saying, "If a white man gives you anything, just remember, when he get ready, he will take it right back" (King, 1982). She believed that self-determination was necessary for Black people.

What we have learned from these three leaders is how they were able to advance the priorities of Black women in electoral and protest politics and elevate the needs of Black women economically, as women working to combat the efforts of white women who have consistently and steadfastly upheld white

---

[60] At the 1976 convention, Jordan said, "We are a people in search of a national community, attempting to fulfill our national purpose, to create a society in which all of us are equal. . . . The great danger America faces [is] that we will cease to be one nation and become instead a collection of interest groups: city against suburb, region against region, individual against individual. Each seeking to satisfy private wants. If that happens, who, then, will speak for America? Who, then, will speak for the common good?"

patriarchy (Junn, 2017). So, what does coalition building look like for Black women in this age, and how can Black women utilize and maximize their power within the Democratic Party at the intersection of race and gender politics? The position of Kamala Harris as the first Black female vice president of the United States has created several debates about the burden of Black female leadership and representation. Black women overperform for the Democratic Party at the local, state, and federal levels. However, even with the contributions of Jordan, Hamer, and Abrams, there is an uncertain future for Black women in the political process – as participants and candidates – where they have been and, in many ways, remain on the outside looking into a house they built.

Stacey Abrams had the audacity to run for a statewide office in the US South, expanding a path paved by politicians like Barbara Jordan and organizers like Fannie Lou Hamer. Abrams built multiracial coalitions and articulated a specific vision of inclusive and active participation for Black American political advancement, similar to those of Ella Baker and Shirley Chisholm before her. As Abrams has written, "Leadership is hard. Convincing others – and often yourself – that you have the answers to overcome long-standing obstacles takes a combination of confidence, insight, and sheer bravado" (2019: xxix–xxx). All three women had to bridge the chasm that separated their talents from the masses of people who refused to see them, purely because of their race and gender.

We must continue to ask ourselves why there have been only two Black female US senators and no Black female governors in the history of the United States. What is it about the audacity of Black women seeking to take the reins of leadership that so many voters cannot fathom or bring themselves to support? How do Black women work around the historical and institutional political barriers that have been put in their paths on statewide levels since the nation's inception? How Hamer, Jordan, and Abrams responded to opportunity and adversity has been the defining characteristic of their political careers. They have left a blueprint for other Black women to follow: an understanding of policy and how it relates to Black people and marginalized groups, the desire to increase electoral participation of Black people, oratorical skills to get one's message across, and coalition building with like-minded individuals and groups. It is my hope that Stacey Abrams and future generations of Black female patriots will continue to chip away at the four pillars of America and add to the structure built by the likes of Fannie Lou Hamer, Barbara Jordan, Shirley Chisholm, Ella Baker, Rosa Parks, and so many other Black women in the US South.

Stacey Abrams's efforts to build coalitions with Black organizations across the South and throughout the United States have possibly created a model for democracy building rooted in increased electoral registration and participation. The Democratic successes in 2020 in Georgia and several other states were real and can be traced directly back to the coalition-building efforts of Abrams. What we do know is that Abrams relies on the words of Fannie Lou Hamer in *Our Time Is Now* to explain our current moment: "We will stay and stand up for what belongs to us as American citizens, because they can't say that we haven't had patience."[61]

---

[61] Opening quote in Abrams (2020).

Bibliography

ABC *Issues and Answers*, with correspondents Bob Clark and Sam Donaldson, July 11, 1976, Barbara Jordan Office Files, LBJ School of Public Affairs, later incorporated into Barbara Jordan Archives, Texas Southern University, Houston.

Abrams, S. (2019). *Lead from the Outside: How to Build Your Future and Make Real Change*. New York: Picador.

Abrams, S. (2020). *Our Time Is Now: Power, Purpose, and the Fight for a Fair America*. New York: Picador.

Abrams, S. (2021). Interviewed by Christina Greer, March 26.

Alex-Assensoh, Y., and A. B. Assensoh (2001). "Inner-City Contexts, Church Attendance and African-American Political Participation." *Journal of Politics*, 63(3): 886–901.

Asch, C. M. (2008). *The Senator and the Sharecropper: The Freedom Struggles of James O. Eastland and Fannie Lou Hamer*. New York: New Press.

Baldwin, J. (1955). *Notes of a Native Son*. New York: Beacon Press.

Barker, L. J., M. H. Jones, and K. Tate (1999). *African Americans and the American Political System*. Upper Saddle River, NJ: Prentice Hall.

Bass, J. and W. De Vries (1975). *The Transformation of Southern Politics: Social Change and Political Consequences since 1945*. New York: Basic.

bell hooks, b. (2004). *We Real Cool: Black Men and Masculinity*. London: Psychology Press.

Berry, D. R. and K. N. Gross (2020). *A Black Women's History of the United States*. Boston, MA: Beacon Press.

Blain, K. N. (2021). *Until I Am Free: Fannie Lou Hamer's Enduring Message to America*. Boston, MA: Beacon Press.

Bracey, E. N. (2011). *Fannie Lou Hamer: The Life of a Civil Rights Icon*. Jefferson, NC: McFarland.

Brooks, M. P. (2014). *A Voice that Could Stir an Army: Fannie Lou Hamer and the Rhetoric of the Black Freedom Movement*. Jackson: University Press of Mississippi.

Brooks, M. P. (2020). *Fannie Lou Hamer: America's Freedom Fighting Women*. New York: Rowman and Littlefield.

Brown, N. E. (2014). *Sisters in the Statehouse: Black Women and Legislative Decision Making*. New York: Oxford University Press.

Brown, N. E. and S. A. Gershon (2016). *Distinct Identities: Minority Women in U.S. Politics*. New York: Routledge Press.

Brown, N. E. and D. C. Lemi (2021). *Sister Style: The Politics of Appearance for Black Women Political Elites*. New York: Oxford University Press.

Brown-Dean, K. L. (2019). *Identity Politics in the United States*. Medford, MA: Polity Press.

Bunch, W. (2021). "Is the Stacey Abrams Method the Only Hope for Saving Democracy in PA?" *The Philadelphia Inquirer*, July 22.

Carroll, S. and K. Sanbonmatsu (2013). *More Women Can Run: Gender and Pathways to the State Legislatures*. New York: Oxford University Press.

Carson, C. (1981). *In Struggle: SNCC and the Black Awakening of the 1960s*. Cambridge, MA: Harvard University Press.

Carter, N. M. (2019). *American while Black: African Americans, Immigration, and the Limits of Citizenship*. New York: Oxford University Press.

Chafe, W., R. Gavins, and R. Korstad (eds.), (2011). *Remembering Jim Crow: African Americans Tell about Life in the Segregated South*. New York: The New Press.

Chisholm, S. ([1970] 2009). *Unbought and Unbossed*. Washington, DC: Take Root Media.

Clarke, J. (1998). "Without Fear or Shame: Lynching, Capital Punishment and the Subculture of Violence in the American South," *British Journal of Political Science*, 28(2): 269–289.

Cohen, C. J. (1999). *The Boundaries of Blackness: AIDS and the Breakdown of Black Politics*. Chicago, IL: University of Chicago Press.

Cohen, C. J. (2003). "A Portrait of Continuing Marginality: The Study of Women of Color in American Politics," in S. J. Carroll (ed.), *Women and American Politics: New Questions, New Directions*. Oxford: Oxford University Press, pp. 190–213.

Cohn, N. (2021). "Why Warnock and Osoff Won in Georgia." *New York Times*, January 8.

Colby, D. (1986). "The Voting Rights Act and Black Registration in Mississippi." *Publius: The Journal of Federalism*, 16(4): 123–138.

Colman, P. (1993). *Fannie Lou Hamer and the Fight for the Vote*. Brookfield, CT: Milbrook Press.

Davis, R. (2020). "Polling Results Estimate 94 Percent of Black Female Voters Chose Hillary Clinton." *Essence*, October 26.

Dawson, M. (1994). "A Black Counterpublic? Economic Earthquakes, Racial Agenda(s), and Black Politics." *Public Culture*, 7(1): 195–223.

Dittmer, J. (1986). "The Politics of the Mississippi Movement 1954–1964," in Charles W. Eagles (ed.), *The Civil Rights Movement in America*. Jackson: University Press of Mississippi.

Dittmer, J. (1994). *Local People: The Struggle for Civil Rights in Mississippi.* Chicago: University of Illinois Press, pp. 65–93.

Donaldson, E. (2017). "Meet Barbara Jordan: Key Influencer in Texas, National Politics." *Community Impact*, February 8.

Donovan, S. (2004). *Fannie Lou Hamer.* Chicago, IL: Raintree Press.

Dowe, P. K. (2020). "Resisting Marginalization: Black Women's Political Ambition and Agency." *PS: Political Science & Politics*, 53(4): 697–702.

Du Bois, W. E. B. ([1935] 1998). *Black Reconstruction in America, 1860–1880.* New York: The Free Press.

Egerton, J. (1970). *A Mind to Stay Here: Profiles from the South.* New York: MacMillan, 1970.

Eschle, C. (2001). *Global Democracy, Social Movements, and Feminism.* New York: Routledge.

Farmer, A. (2017). *Remaking Black Political Power: How Black Women Transformed an Era.* Chapel Hill: University of North Carolina Press.

Foner, E. (2014). *Reconstruction: America's Unfinished Revolution, 1863–1877.* New York: Harper Perennial Modern Classics.

Ford, T. C. (2015). *Liberated Threads: Black Women, Style, and the Global Politics of Soul.* Chapel Hill: University of North Carolina Press.

Francis, M. M. (2019). "The Price of Civil Rights: Black Politics, White Money, and Movement Capture." *Law & Society Review*, 53(1): 275–309.

Franklin, S. (2014). *After the Rebellion: Black Youth, Social Movement Activism, and the Post-Civil Rights Generation.* New York: New York University Press.

Frymer, P. (1999). *Uneasy Alliances: Race and Party Competition in America.* Princeton, NJ: Princeton University Press.

Garland, P. (1966). "Builders of a New South." *Ebony*, August, pp. 27–37.

Garrison, T. A. (2009). *The Legal Ideology of Removal: The Southern Judiciary and the Sovereignty of Native American Nations.* Athens: University of Georgia Press.

Gay, C. and K. Tate (1998). "Doubly Bound: The Impact of Gender and Race on the Politics of Black Women." *Political Psychology*, 19(1): 169–184.

Gershon, S. A., C. Montoya, C. Bejarano, & N. Brown. (2019). "Intersectional Linked Fate and Political Representation." *Politics, Groups, and Identities*, 7(3): 642–653.

Giddings, P. (1975). "Will the Real Barbara Jordan Please Stand." *Encore American & Worldwide News*, May 9.

Gillespie, A. (2010). *Whose Black Politics? Cases in Post-Racial Black Leadership.* New York: Routledge Press.

Gillespie, A. (2012). *The New Black Politician: Cory Booker, Newark, and Post-Racial America.* New York: New York University Press.

Goodyear, D. (2020). "Kamala Harris Makes History." *New Yorker*, November 8.

Grant, K. N. (2020). *The Great Migration and the Democratic Party: Black Voters and the Realignment of American Politics in the 20th Century.* Philadelphia, PA: Temple University Press.

Greer, C. M. (2013). *Black Ethnics: Race, Immigration, and the Pursuit of the American Dream.* New York: Oxford University Press.

Greer, C. M. (2016a). "To Be Young, Gifted, Black, and a Woman: A Comparison of the Presidential Candidacies of Charlene Mitchell and Shirley Chisholm," in N. E. Brown and S. A. Gershon (eds.), *Distinct Identities: Minority Women in U.S. Politics.* New York: Routledge Press, pp. 252–267.

Greer, C. M. (2016b). "African-American Candidates for the Presidency and the Foundation of Black Politics in the Twenty-First Century." *Politics, Groups, and Identities*, 4(4): 638–651.

Greer, C. M. (2018a). "If Anyone Can Be America's First Black Woman Governor, It's Stacey Abrams." *Daily Beast*, April 24.

Greer, C. M. (2018b). "Hart-Celler and the Effects on African American and Immigrant Incorporation." *National Political Science Review*, 19(1): 14–28.

Guild, J. (2009). "To Make that Someday Come," in D. F. Gore, J. Theoharis, and K. Woodard (eds.), *Want to Start a Revolution? Black Women in the Black Freedom Struggle.* New York: New York University Press, pp. 248–270.

Guinier, L. and G. Torres (2002). *The Miner's Canary: Enlisting Race, Resisting Power, Transforming Democracy.* Cambridge, MA: Harvard University Press.

Hamer, F. L. (1966). Foreword to T. Sugarman, *Stranger at the Gates: A Summer in Mississippi.* New York: Hill and Wang.

Hamer, F. L. (1981). "Mississippi Movement: Interview with Ella Jo Baker and Fannie Lou Hamer." *Southern Exposure*, 9(1): 47.

Hancock, A. (2004). *The Politics of Disgust: The Public Identity of the Welfare Queen.* New York: New York University Press.

Harris-Perry, M. V. (2013). *Sister Citizen: Shame, Stereotypes, and Black Women in America.* New Haven, CT: Yale University Press.

Hayes, F. W. (2000). *A Turbulent Voyage: Readings in African American Studies.* San Diego, CA: Collegiate Press.

Herbers, J. (1964). "Communiqué from the Mississippi Front." *New York Times*, November 8.

Hicks, H. (2022). "Intersectional Stereotyping in Media Coverage: The Case of Stacey Abrams and Stacey Evans in Georgia." *Journal of Women, Politics, & Policy*, 43(1): 95–106.

Hilt, J. (2015). "There Are No Survivors without Scars." *Bitch Media*, August 26, www.bitchmedia.org/article/there-are-no-survivors-without-scars.

Hine, D. C. and K. Thompson (1999). *A Shining Thread of Hope: The History of Black Women in America*. New York: Broadway.

Hinojosa, M. and M. Kittilson. (2020). *Seeing Women, Strengthening Democracy: How Women in Politics Foster Connected Citizens*. New York: Oxford University Press.

Hooker, J. (2017). "Black Protest/White Grievance: On the Problem of White Political Imaginations Not Shaped by Loss," *South Atlantic Quarterly*, 116(3): 483–504.

hooks, b. (1997). Interview in *Cultural Criticism & Transformation* by Sut Jhally, Media Education Foundation, Northampton, MA, www.mediaed.org/transcripts/Bell-Hooks-Transcript.pdf.

Howell, S. and C. Day (2000). "Complexities of the Gender Gap," *Journal of Politics*, 62(3): 858–874.

Johnson, J. M. (2020). *Wicked Flesh: Black Women, Intimacy, and Freedom in the Atlantic World*. Philadelphia: University of Pennsylvania Press.

Johnson, M. E. (2018). "The Paradox of Black Patriotism: Double Consciousness." *Ethnic and Racial Studies*, 41(11): 1971–1989.

Jones, M. S. (2020). *Vanguard: How Black Women Broke Barriers, Won the Vote, and Insisted on Equality for All*. New York: Basic Elements.

Jordan, B. (1975). *Extension of the Voting Rights Act: Hearings before the House Judiciary Committee, Subcommittee on Civil and Constitutional Rights*, 94th Cong., 1st sess., Serial No. 1, pts. 1 and 2, February 25–March 25, p. 77.

Jordan, B. (1990). "Looking for a Vision for the 1990s," remarks at a Great Society Roundup, LBJ Presidential Library, Austin, Texas, May 5.

Jordan, B. (1995). "The Americanization Ideal." *New York Times*, September 11.

Jordan, J. (1972). *Fannie Lou Hamer*. New York: Thomas Y. Crowell.

Jordan-Zachery, J. S. (2009). *Black Women, Cultural Images and Social Policy*. New York: Routledge.

Junn, J. (2017). "2016 Election Reflection Series: Hiding in Plain Sight: White Women Vote Republican." *Political Science Now*, December 23.

Kammer, J. (2016). "Remembering Barbara Jordan and Her Immigration Legacy." *Center for Immigration Studies*, January 17, pp. 1–7.

Kaplan, T. (2004). *Taking Back the Streets: Women, Youth, and Direct Democracy*. Oakland: University of California Press.

Kaufmann, K. (2006). "The Gender Gap." *PS: Political Science*, 39(3): 447–453.

King, E. (1982). "Go Tell It on the Mountain: A Prophet from the Delta." *Sojourners (Dec. 1982)*, 18, 21.

King, M. (1975). "Oppression and Power: The Unique Status of Black Women in the American Political System." *Social Science Quarterly*, 56(1): 117–128.

Klein, G. (1994). "Cost of Illegal Immigration Is High." *Richmond Times-Dispatch*, April 17.

Kling, S. (1979). *Fannie Lou Hamer: A Biography*. Chicago, IL: Women for Racial and Economic Equality.

Lanker, B. (1989). *I Dream a World*. New York: Stewart, Tabori, & Chang.

Larson, K. C. (2021). *Walk with Me: A Biography of Fannie Lou Hamer*. New York: Oxford University Press.

Lee, C. K. (1999). *For Freedom's Sake: The Life of Fannie Lou Hamer*. Chicago: University of Illinois Press.

Lemi, D. and N. Brown (2020). "The Political Implications of Colorism Are Gendered." *PS: Political Science & Politics*, 53(4): 669–673.

Lerner, L. and S. Ember (2020). "Kamala Harris Makes History as First Woman and Woman of Color as VP." *New York Times*, November 7.

Lijphart, A. (1997). "Unequal Participation: Democracy's Unresolved Dilemma Presidential Address: APSA 1996." *American Political Science Review*, 91(1): 1–14.

Lithwick, D. (2019). "The Irony of Modern Feminism's Obsession with Ruth Bader Ginsburg." *Atlantic*, January/February.

McGhee, H. (2021). *The Sum of Us: What Racism Costs Everyone When We Can Prosper Together*. New York: One World.

McLemore, L. B. (1971). "The Mississippi Freedom Democratic Party: A Case Study of Grassroots Politics." PhD dissertation, University of Massachusetts, Amherst.

Metzl, J. M. (2019). *Dying of Whiteness: How the Politics of Racial Resentment Is Killing America's Heartland*. New York: Basic Elements.

Michener, J. (2018). *Fragmented Democracy: Medicaid, Federalism, and Unequal Politics*. New York: Cambridge University Press.

Mickey, R. (2015). *Paths Out of Dixie: The Democratization of Authoritarian Enclaves in America's Deep South, 1944–1972*. Princeton, NJ: Princeton University Press.

Minor, B. (2006). "Hamer at '64 Dem Convention Fueled Miss. Party's Defection." *Clarion-Ledger*, February 26.

Newman, R. and M. Sawyer (1996). *Everybody Say Freedom: Everything You Need to Know about African-American History*. New York: A Plume Element.

Noe-Bustamante, L. and A. Budiman (2020). "Black, Latino and Asian Americans Have Been Key to Georgia's Registered Voter Growth since 2016." *Pew Research Center*, December 21.

O'Dell, J. (1965). "Life in Mississippi: An Interview with Fannie Lou Hamer." *Freedomways*, 2nd Quarter.

Olsen, M. (1972). "Social Participation and Voting Turnout: A Multivariate Analysis." *American Sociological Review*, 37(3): 317–333.

Page, B. and R. Shapiro. (1993). *The Rational Public and Democracy*. Chicago, IL: University of Chicago Press.

Painter, N. (2021). *Southern History across the Color Line*. Chapel Hill: University of North Carolina Press.

Parker, F. (2011). *Black Votes Count: Political Empowerment in Mississippi after 1965*. Chapel Hill: University of North Carolina Press.

Pew Research Center (2016). "On Views of Race and Inequality, Blacks and Whites Are Worlds Apart." June 27. www.pewresearch.org/wp-content/uploads/sites/20/2016/06/ST_2016.06.27_Race-Inequality-Final.pdf

Qin, Y. (2023). "Grassroots Governance and Social Development: Theoretical and Comparative Legal Aspects." *Humanities and Social Sciences Communications*, 10(1): 331.

Randolph, S. M. (2009). "Women's Liberation or . . . Black Liberation, You're Fighting the Same Enemies," in D. Gore, J. Theoharis, and K. Woodard (eds.), *Want to Start a Revolution? Black Women in the Black Freedom Struggle*. New York: New York University Press, pp. 223–247.

Ransby, B. (2003). *Ella Baker and the Black Freedom Movement: A Radical Democratic Vision*. Chapel Hill: University of North Carolina Press.

Reed, L. (1993). "Fannie Lou Hamer (1917–1977)," in D. C. Hine, E. Barkley Brown, and R. Terborg-Penn (eds.), *Black Women in America: An Historical Encyclopedia*. Indianapolis: Indiana University Press.

Reeves, J. (2017). "In Poor Black Belt Region, Both Fears and Prayers over Trump." *Associated Press*. February 25.

Rhodes, J. (2003). "Black Radicalism in 1960s California: Women in the Black Panther Party," in Q. Taylor and S. A. Wilson Moore (eds.), *African American Women Confront the West, 1600–2000*. Norman: University of Oklahoma Press, pp. 346–362.

Rogers, M. B. (1998). *Barbara Jordan: American Hero*. New York: Bantam Elements.

Rubel, D. (1990). *Fannie Lou Hamer: From Sharecropping to Politics*. New York: Silver Burdett.

Sanders, C. L. (1975). "Barbara Jordan, Texan, Is a New Power on Capitol Hill." *Ebony*, February.

Sewell, G. (1978). "Fannie Lou Hamer." *Black Collegian*, May/June, p. 20.

Sherman, M. (ed.), (2007). *Barbara Jordan: Speaking the Truth with Eloquent Thunder*. Austin: University of Texas Press.

Simien, E. M. (2006). *Black Feminist Voices in Politics*. New York: State University of New York Press.

Slaughter, C., C. Crowder, and C. Greer (2024). "Black Women: Keepers of Democracy, the Democratic Process, and the Democratic Party." *Politics & Gender*, 20(1): 162–181.

Smooth, W. (2011). "Standing for Women? Which Women? The Substantive Representation of Women's Interests and the Research Imperative of Intersectionality." *Politics & Gender*, 7(3): 436–441.

Smooth, W. (2014). "African American Women and Electoral Politics: Translating Voting Power into Office Holding," in S. J. Carroll and R. L. Fox (eds.), *Gender and Elections: Shaping the Future of American Politics* (3rd edition). New York: Cambridge University Press, pp. 167–189.

Spritzer, L. N. and J. B. Bergmark (2009). *Grace Towns Hamilton and the Politics of Southern Change*. Athens: University of Georgia Press.

Stokes-Brown, A. K. and K. Dolan (2010). "Race, Gender, and Symbolic Representation: African American Female Candidates as Mobilizing Agents." *Journal of Elections, Public Opinion and Parties*, 20(4): 473–494.

Stoper, E. (1977). "The Student Nonviolent Coordinating Committee: Rise and Fall of a Redemptive Organization." *Journal of Black Studies*, 8(1): 18.

Tate, K. (1998). *From Protest to Politics*. Cambridge, MA: Harvard University Press.

Tillery, Jr., A. B. (2011). *Between Homeland and Motherland: Africa, U.S. Foreign Policy, and Black Leadership in America*. Ithaca, NY: Cornell University Press.

Timpone, R. (1997). "The Voting Rights Act and Electoral Empowerment: The Case of Mississippi." *Social Science Quarterly*, 78(1): 177–185.

Walsh, J. (2018). "Stacey Abrams Makes History." *The Nation*, May 23.

Walton, H. (1985). *Invisible Politics: Black Political Behavior*. New York: SUNY Press.

Walton, Jr., H., P. K. Ford Dowe, and J. A. V. Allen (2016). *Remaking the Democratic Party: Lyndon B. Johnson as a Native-Son Presidential Candidate*. Ann Arbor: University of Michigan Press.

Waxman, O. (2020). "Stacey Abrams and Other Georgia Organizers Are Part of a Long – but Often Overlooked – Tradition of Black Women Working for the Vote." *Time*, November 10.

Weigel, D. (2014). "Can Georgia Democrats Make the State Turn Blue Ahead of Schedule?" *Slate*, May 19.

Williams, J. (1987). *Eyes on the Prize: America's Civil Rights Years, 1954–1965*. New York: Penguin Press.

Williams, R. F. (1960). "Can Negroes Afford to Be Pacifists?" *New Left Review*, 1 (January/February): 44–46.

Wirls, D. (1986). "Reinterpreting the Gender Gap," *Public Opinion Quarterly*, 50(3): 316–330.

Young, A. (1996). *An Easy Burden: The Civil Rights Movement and Transformation of America*. New York: Harper Collins.

Race, Ethnicity, and Politics

Megan Ming Francis
University of Washington

Megan Ming Francis is the G. Alan and Barbara Delsman Associate Professor of Political Science at the University of Washington and a Fellow at the Ash Center for Democratic Governance and the Carr Center for Human Rights at the Harvard Kennedy School. Francis is the author of the award winning book, *Civil Rights and the Making of the Modern American State*. She is particularly interested in American political and constitutional development, social movements, the criminal punishment system, Black politics, philanthropy, and the post-Civil War South.

About the Series

Elements in Race, Ethnicity, and Politics is an innovative publishing initiative in the social sciences. The series publishes important original research that breaks new ground in the study of race, ethnicity, and politics. It welcomes research that speaks to the current political moment, research that provides new perspectives on established debates, and interdisciplinary research that sheds new light on previously understudied topics and groups.

Cambridge Elements $\equiv$

Race, Ethnicity, and Politics

Elements in the Series

Walls, Cages, and Family Separation: Race and Immigration Policy in the Trump Era
Sophia Jordán Wallace, Chris Zepeda-Millán

*(Mis)Informed: What Americans Know About Social Groups and Why
it Matters for Politics*
Marisa Abrajano, Nazita Lajevardi

Racial Order, Racialized Responses: Interminority Politics in a Diverse Nation
Efrén O. Pérez, E. Enya Kuo

*Which Lives Matter?: Factors Shaping Public Attention to and Protest
of Officer-Involved Killings*
Traci Burch

Women Voters: Race, Gender, and Dynamism in American Elections
Jane Junn, Natalie Masuoka

*How to Build a Democracy: From Fannie Lou Hamer and Barbara Jordan
to Stacey Abrams*
Christina M. Greer

A full series listing is available at: www.cambridge.org/EREP

Printed in the United States
by Baker & Taylor Publisher Services